Shepherds of the Desert

Shepherds of the Desert

David Keith Jones

ELM TREE BOOKS · LONDON

To Carla, Mark and Katherine
who travelled with me

Endpapers This huge open landscape south of the
Huri Hills is typical grazing country for the nomadic
Gabbra herds

Title page Rendille children watching the sunset

Above Men and women co-operate to water this
huge herd of camels and goats at a man-made
waterhole near Kalkacha, south of Moyale on the
road to Wajir

Previous page The vast stony desert north of the
'village of two houses' near Maikona. Thirty miles
away the Huri Hills notch the horizon

First published in Great Britain 1984
by Elm Tree Books/Hamish Hamilton Ltd
Garden House, 57–59 Long Acre, London WC2E 9JZ

Copyright © 1984 by David Keith Jones

Book design by Alan Hamp
Maps conceived by the author and drawn by Patrick Leeson

British Library Cataloguing in Publication Data
Jones, David Keith
    Shepherds of the desert.
    1. Nomads—Kenya—Pictorial works
    I. Title
    967.6´204   GN635.K/

    ISBN 0-241-10349-5

Filmset and printed in Great Britain
by Jolly & Barber Ltd, Rugby

Contents

Acknowledgements

In 15,000 miles of desert travel through northern Kenya I have been helped by countless people. Some have offered hospitality, some given good advice; others have done both and become close friends.

Many people have helped me with ideas, insights and understandings, some in conversations, others through their writings. Without wishing to claim scholarly authority for a book which is essentially a personal impression I am particularly grateful to Anne W. Beaman, Jean Brown, Leslie Brown, Lester R. Brown, Malcolm B. Collins, Jean Colvin, Dr Dyson-Hudson, Erik Eckholm, A.C. Field, C.R. Field, Anders Grum, P.H. Gulliver, Mary Hook, George Kiragu, H. Kruuk, Hugh Lamprey, Richard Leakey, Walter Lusigi, Paul Robinson, Paul Spencer, Fr Paolo Tablino.

For hospitality and guidance in remote places I would like to thank Fr Luigi Andeni, 'Dilly' Anderson, Neil Bradshaw, Fr Cornelio, Rodney Elliott, Iltirim Gambare and his wife Yelowa, Fr Giuffre, Pius Godana, Dick Hedges, Simon Karabu, Peter Kona, Fr Matthew, Br Mario, Julian McKeand, Fr Moruzzi, Samuel Labarakwe, John Oche, Fr Pellerino, Fr Giuseppe Ronchi, Paul Smith, Fr Thomas, Lufle Gambare Torder and Jeiso Wambile.

Obviously my greatest debt is to the many nomads who tolerated my cameras with good humour and invited me into their homes. May this book be a tribute to them.

Introduction

Nairobi, just $1\frac{1}{4}$ degrees south of the equator, is the twentieth century's child. Airports, hotels, industries, schools, housing estates, even the cardboard shanty towns, have all sprung up since 1900; the unintended progeny of the first cluster of huts, spawned by the railhead as it raced to the great lake carrying boats and dreams for Uganda.

In Nairobi today, a mile above the sea, the telex machines are busy, the parking spaces are full and almost a million people wrestle with the problems of the 1980s. Drive north, out of the city, and you are soon in farming country: in the first hundred miles, coffee, tea, pineapples, maize, bananas, cattle, villages, towns, farms all flit by at the side of the tarmac road. Then a sign for the equator, with stalls selling trinkets to tourists, and the road climbs the shoulder of Mount Kenya through wheat and barley fields with glimpses of high glaciers hanging from the towering peaks.

Here, struggling in the thin air at almost 9,000 feet, the car loses power until suddenly the road is descending, dropping, falling into a huge, empty vista, broken on the far horizon by distant threads of blue hills.

Now, as you gather speed down the long slope towards the dry country, your car becomes a time-machine carrying you out of the twentieth century, back into the vast ancient spaces of traditional Africa. Symbolically, at Isiolo, there is a barrier and the tarmac road turns into dirt; in the next miles men with spears step aside to avoid your dust.

There are other routes into the great semi-deserts of northern Kenya; but each brings the traveller to a point in the land where the dry country ahead appears as an ocean seen from the hinterland. Like an ocean the desert announces itself from afar, not merely as a view of shimmering distances, but by a new feel to the air, new scents, new sounds, a changing quality of light. This feeling of moving down into a different world is no illusion; for desert dwellers, like mariners, must master exacting skills and disciplines or perish. For countless millennia a sprinkling of tough, self-reliant nomads has lived in the huge arid lands of northern Kenya. Needing nothing and caring nothing for the outside world they have wandered with their herds, made their own artefacts, sung their own songs, created customs and societies.

In this book I hope to show something of the traditions and ways of life of these extraordinary shepherds of the desert; and to record some of the timeless, often breathtakingly beautiful landscapes where they roam.

The Land

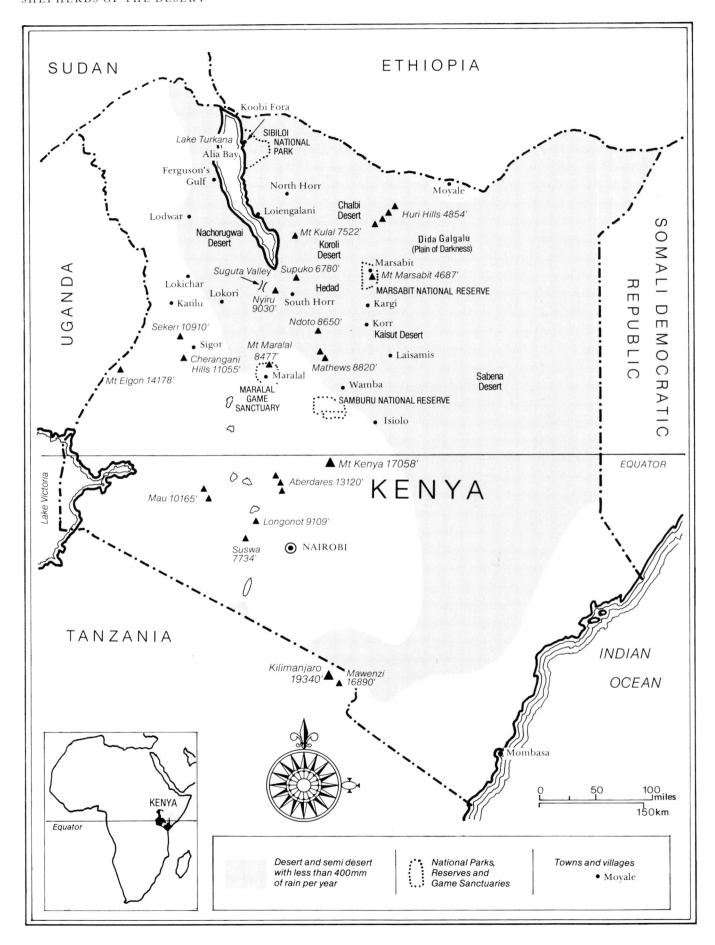

SUDAN

ETHIOPIA

UGANDA

SOMALI DEMOCRATIC REPUBLIC

Koobi Fora

Lake Turkana
Alia Bay

SIBILOI
NATIONAL
PARK

Ferguson's
Gulf

North Horr

Moyale

Lodwar

Loiengalani

Chalbi
Desert

▲ Huri Hills 4854'

Nachorugwai
Desert

▲ Mt Kulal 7522'

Dida Galgalu
(Plain of Darkness)

Koroli
Desert

Suguta Valley

Supuko 6780'

Marsabit

Lokichar

Lokori

▲ Mt Marsabit 4687'

MARSABIT NATIONAL RESERVE

Hedad

Katilu

*Nyiru
9030'*

South Horr

• Kargi

Sekerr 10910'

Ndoto 8650'

• Korr

Kaisut Desert

Sigor

*Mt Maralal
8477'*

• Laisamis

*Cherangani
Hills 11055'*

▲

Mathews 8820'

Sabena
Desert

▲ *Mt Elgon 14178'*

Maralal

• Wamba

MARALAL
GAME
SANCTUARY

SAMBURU NATIONAL RESERVE

• Isiolo

Lake Victoria

▲ Mt Kenya 17058'

EQUATOR

▲ Aberdares 13120'

KENYA

Mau 10165'

▲ *Longonot 9109'*

⊙ NAIROBI

*Suswa
7734'*

TANZANIA

INDIAN

OCEAN

*Kilimanjaro
19340'*

*Mawenzi
16890'*

• Mombasa

KENYA

Equator

0   50   100
                    miles
150km

Desert and semi desert
with less than 400mm
of rain per year

National Parks,
Reserves and
Game Sanctuaries

Towns and villages
• Moyale

KENYA'S TOTAL LAND AREA is 224,000 square miles; but 88% is classed as arid, or semi-arid, with a rainfall of less than 24 inches a year, the minimum needed in Africa to till the land and grow crops without irrigation.

In East Africa, apart from a ten-mile coastal strip, climate depends upon altitude, for the higher lands create rain. Thus in Kenya almost all successful development has occurred above 3500 feet and much of the country's best farmland is more than twice this high. Apart from the port of Mombasa and one or two coastal towns all major centres are well above sea-level, with Nairobi, the capital city, at around 5500 feet.

Since the major tracts of high ground are in southern and western Kenya this is where most people live and where roads and railways have opened up the country to modern trade and influences. Out of the total population of roughly 17 million, around 16 million live in the southern half of Kenya; even here there are large areas of dry country, some of which have been made into National Parks and Reserves like Tsavo and Amboseli. But northern Kenya is almost all dry, the only exception being a few isolated mountain peaks which create a little local rain and so are clothed in mist forest. The remainder of the north is low-lying and is thus part of the huge swathe of arid land which stretches 3000 miles across Africa, just south of the Sahara. This is the kingdom of the nomad.

The semi-desert northern half of Kenya has an area of 108,000 square miles, which makes it larger that Great Britain, Italy or New Zealand; but its population density is one of the lowest in the world and it is a vast and open land. Here there are no permanent rivers, no power lines and no tarmac roads (although the first is under construction on the west side of Lake Turkana to create a trading link with Sudan). In the east, towards Somalia, it can be flat and dull; during a 600-mile drive from Moyale on the Ethiopian border, south through Wajir and Garissa to Garsen and Malindi on the Kenya coast, we drove for two days through a monotonous corridor of grey bush. But further west the land is riven by the Great Rift Valley and seems to have an almost muscular energy of its own.

Here sweeping valleys and open plains are punctuated by dramatic peaks and the eye is constantly pulled to the furthest horizons where distant mountains promise yet more views beyond. So empty is this landscape that it seems to expand the mind; there is constant variety and an unyielding sense of space so that the traveller seems to be moving through a kind of symphony of land. For hours the only sign of man is the unrolling ribbon of track, dipping and curving ahead into a timeless primeval landscape; there is a feeling of driving back towards the origins of the earth into a time before agriculture and before the wheel.

In fact this is a paradox, for the rugged region of northern Kenya is geologically new. The flat land, in the north-east of Kenya, is made up of shield rocks roughly 3000 million years old which have had more than enough time to erode down to a monotonous sameness; hence our long dull drive from Moyale to the coast. These shield rocks are amongst the oldest known, more than five times the age of Cambrian rocks which are an important 'time-stone' for geologists since they mark the beginning of the

Previous page Spectacular rock formations in Sibiloi National Park

13

Wind has crafted the exquisite curves of these sand dunes at Bosgobo, north west of the Chalbi Desert

Palaeozoic age when the first forms of life appeared. But although, at 570 million years, Cambrian rocks are a mere fraction of the age of shield rocks, yet they are immensely old in comparison with parts of north-west Kenya, some of which are practically brand new geologically, for it is here that the Great Rift Valley has tumbled the land into dramatic scenery.

The largest single geological feature of the earth's surface, the Great Rift Valley, stretches 4000 miles from Lebanon to Mozambique and has all been created in the last 20 million years. Indeed the process of change continues today, for there is still plenty of volcanic activity. Hot springs and fumaroles occur in many places and the first European to visit the area, Count Teleki, gave his name to a new volcano at the southern end of Lake Turkana which, although active in 1888, has since almost disappeared.

There are many spectacular and thrilling viewpoints into the Rift in both southern and northern Kenya and in other countries further north and south; but the view from Lesiolo on Maralal mountain is outstanding. Maralal is the administrative capital of Samburu district, a strange wild-west style town clinging to the edge of a range of volcanic hills which form an island in the semi-deserts. North of the town a dirt road climbs fiercely through cedar forests on to a windswept, cool plateau, then rises yet again to reach a sudden crest at over 8000 feet. From here the road drops steeply to the north, back into the desert plains; but from the crest a spur of land carries a motorable track westwards to the end of an airy peninsula which juts above the void. Here towering cliffs drop into a distorted, quivering landscape strewn with volcanic hills. Cones join with cones to form serried ranks marching across the Rift Valley floor towards the Cherengani Hills. Here it seems as though a geological time-lapse camera has been made to run backwards and stopped a mere handful of frames before the beginning of the earth. Over and over again in northern Kenya there is the feeling of having fallen unconsciously into a time-machine, only to emerge and see for oneself how things were in the distant past.

75 miles north of Lesiolo an even newer landscape offers text book examples of volcanic change at the southern end of Lake Turkana.

In 1888 when Count Teleki and his assistant von Höhnel became the first Europeans to reach this lake it was known to the local people as Basso Narok. But Teleki decided to call it Lake Rudolf in honour of Prince Rudolf of Austria, who had taken a keen interest in Teleki's privately organised expedition. Then, following Kenya's independence in 1963, the lake was renamed again after the tough Turkana people who live on its western and southern shores.

160 miles long and 30 wide, Lake Turkana is the largest alkaline lake in the world and is an astonishing anachronism in its setting of surrounding deserts. Fed by the Omo river, which drains Ethiopian highlands to the north, and by seasonal rivers from Kenya's mountains to the south, the lake is nevertheless drying out and may once have been four times its present size. Sodium carbonate, from the volcanic rocks of the area, gives its waters a brackish taste and encourages the growth of algae giving the lake its characteristic green colour and popular name, the Jade Sea. These spirulina algae are the basic diet of Lesser Flamingoes, often seen on the lake in big numbers. And the same algae form the base of a food chain which includes fish, crocodiles and many water birds.

It is at the southern end of the lake that the volcanoes are most obvious. Here they form a barrier preventing water draining away into the low-lying furnace of the Suguta Valley. Lake Turkana itself has a low altitude by East African standards, the surface being just 1200 feet above sea-level; but on the other side of the barrier the ground drops down to a mere 825 feet making it the lowest, and probably the hottest, place in inland Kenya. The tangled mass of peaks and rocks which forms this natural dam is an appalling place and makes one thankful for the softening curves which erosion brings. But as an object lesson on the bones of the earth it can have few equals. Black lava fields and cinder cones litter the landscape which is almost devoid of vegetation. To walk across this country is close to purgatory; but seen from the air it is awe-inspiring. The most spectacular peak of all in this frighteningly raw land has erupted out of the lake itself. With poetic, albeit gruesome simile, the Turkana have named this perfectly symmetrical cone *Nabuyaton* – 'the elephant's stomach' – doubtless inspired by the huge lava fields which the volcano has vomited to the south, engulfing many square miles of lake and shore.

The first Europeans didn't think much of this area either. In most parts of the world a large body of water like Lake Turkana would be the centre of lush and fertile land, and naturally this is what Count Teleki and his party expected as they journeyed towards Basso Narok. Indeed when they were a mere two days march from the lake and a native asked them what they intended to do with their cattle, 'for there is not a blade of grass near it', the explorers gave him a disbelieving smile! But here is von Höhnel, Teleki's assistant, writing of their last few hours struggling towards the lake shore, the culmination of a thirteen month march covering over 800 miles:

'The mountain district between us and the lake was, in fact, a veritable hell, consisting of a series of parallel heights, running from north to south, which we had to cut across in a north-westerly direction. The slopes of these mountains were steep precipices, most of them quite insurmountable, and those that were not were strewn with blackish-brown blocks of rock or of loose sharp-edged scoriae. The narrow valleys were encumbered with stones, or debris, or with loose deep sand in which our feet sunk, making progress difficult. And when the sun rose higher, its rays were reflected from the smooth brownish-black surface of the rock, causing an almost intolerable glare, whilst a burning wind from the south whirled sand in our faces, and almost blew the loads off the heads of the men.

Almost at our last gasp, we hastened on towards the slightly rippled sheet of water – the one bit of brightness in a gloomy scene. Another hour of tramping through sand or over stony flats, and we were at the shore of the lake. Although utterly exhausted, after the seven hours' march in the intense and parching heat, we felt our spirits rise once more as we stood upon the beach at last, and saw the beautiful water, clear as crystal, stretching away before us. The men rushed down shouting, to plunge into the lake: but soon returned in bitter disappointment: the water was brackish!

This defeat of all our expectations was like a revelation to us: and like some threatening spectre rose up before our minds the full significance of the utterly barren, dreary nature of the lake district. Into what a desert had we been betrayed! A few scattered tufts of fine stiff grass rising up in melancholy fashion near the shore, from the wide stretches of sand, were the only bits of green, the only signs of life of any kind. Here and there, some partly in the water, some on the beach, rose up isolated skeletons of trees, stretching up their bare sun-bleached branches to the pitiless sky. No living creature shared the gloomy solitude with us: and far as our glass could reach there was nothing to be seen but desert – desert everywhere. To all this was added the scorching heat, and the ceaseless buffeting of the sand-laden wind, against which we were powerless to protect ourselves upon the beach, which offered not a scrap of shelter, whilst the pitching of the tents in the loose sand was quite impossible.'

Anyone who has travelled from South Horr to Loiengalani on the south-east shores of Lake Turkana will recognise von Höhnel's vivid description, for this area has hardly changed in the last hundred years. A rough stony track, barely suitable for Land-Rovers and other four-wheel drive vehicles, is the only concession the twentieth century has so far wrung out of this unyielding

The beautiful peaks of Baio on the edge of the Kaisut Desert

landscape. And yet, in his disappointment in not reaching a lush green land, in his anxiety to make clear the undoubtedly serious situation in which the expedition found itself, von Höhnel chose, in the passage quoted, to ignore the savage beauty of this place. Von Höhnel's impression that he was looking at a vacant landscape may also have been at fault. True the shoreline was empty as his party arrived; I too have seen those beaches desolate and void of life except for a few blades of grass. But on another day there may come a hundred, or a thousand camels with tall black men and slim lithe girls. For an hour the air is full of their voices and the camels bellowing cries until, after all have drunk and the gourds are filled, away they stride, back into the stony hills leaving no trace upon the shore.

In northern Kenya man inhabits the barren ground without necessarily showing himself from afar; and it seems to me essential to set the lives of the African pastoralists properly against the background of their harsh environment. For this is not a region where western man can arrive with pre-packed schemes to change the world. Indeed a distressing number of well-meaning projects designed to improve life in northern Kenya have come to grief since Teleki and von Höhnel struggled to the lake. And while it may well be that scientists will eventually create some truly worthwhile changes it seems to me that the greatest triumphs man has had so far in these broad, dry lands are the triumphs of those wandering shepherds of the desert, the Pokot, Turkana, Samburu, Gabbra and Rendille people who have tuned their social systems and their skills to harmonise with the slow, harsh rhythms of their nomad's world.

17

Left Running north from the Ndoto Mountains this seasonal stream flows into the desert plains. An abandoned Rendille settlement, or *gob*, in the foreground testifies that water can be found here following rain in the hills

Below The volcanic cone of Nabuyaton — Turkana for 'the elephant's stomach' — at the southern end of Lake Turkana

Above Looking down the Larachi Gorge from the 7000 foot southern summit of Mount Kulal towards the distant gleam of Lake Turkana. Exposed layers of rock show the mountain's volcanic origin. Now protected by UNESCO's World Heritage Convention, Mount Kulal is clothed in mist forest and inhabited by Samburu people

Overleaf 'For hours the only sign of man is the unrolling ribbon of track, dipping and curving ahead into a timeless primeval landscape.' Here we are looking towards Illim and the Milgis lugga from the Kaisut Desert

Life in
the Desert

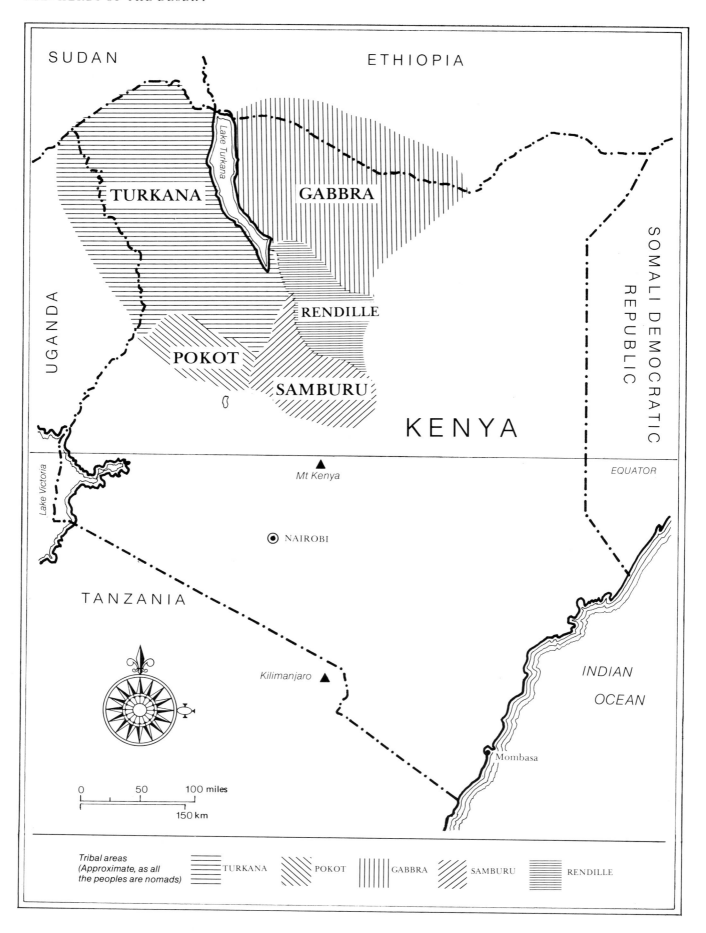

SUDAN

ETHIOPIA

Lake Turkana

TURKANA

GABBRA

UGANDA

RENDILLE

POKOT

SOMALI DEMOCRATIC REPUBLIC

SAMBURU

KENYA

Mt Kenya

EQUATOR

◉ NAIROBI

Lake Victoria

TANZANIA

INDIAN

OCEAN

Kilimanjaro ▲

0   50   100 miles

150 km

Mombasa

Tribal areas
(Approximate, as all
the peoples are nomads)   TURKANA   POKOT   GABBRA   SAMBURU   RENDILLE

THERE ARE NO permanent rivers in the northern half of Kenya. Between the Uaso Nyiro (which flows across the Laikipia plateau and through Samburu National Reserve) and the Ethiopian border there are over 108,000 square miles of dry country; and yet the people who live there do not consider themselves to be short of water.

Although throughout the region there are less than 15 inches of rain a year, when rain does come it can be torrential, in the form of thunderstorms. Indeed the lower the annual rainfall the more capricious the climate; sometimes a whole year's rain may fall in two or three heavy storms; sometimes the rain may fail altogether. Statistically the variation is astonishing: as much as 1200% change between one year and another is possible in semi-desert country!

After a storm tiny streams turn into raging torrents and flash floods form a rushing wall of water down dry river beds which sweep trees away like weeds. Occasionally a luckless traveller will be caught half way across a dry river bed when he is overwhelmed by the result of a thunderstorm far away in the hills; even four-wheel drive lorries can be overturned or carried downstream.

Water may flow for a few days, perhaps even for a few weeks. Then it will shrink to a trickle, to a mere stain in the ground and a week later there is only a broad sandy gully, fringed by trees, a typical *lugga* of northern Kenya. For months afterwards the larger trees will stay green, proving they are drawing water from under the sand. It is this underground water which is the main supply for the nomads; they know the best places in the dry stream beds to dig and after each storm the wells will be re-opened. At first a shallow hole will be sufficient but as the dry season lengthens they must work deeper, sometimes going down over 50 feet.

From such a well water must be lifted by hand, often in buckets fashioned from giraffe hide – a tough leather that can last twenty years – into hollow wooden troughs from which the animals drink. To water a big herd may take several hours and is probably the heaviest routine task in the nomad's life. And yet it is a fact that shortage of water is not the people of the desert's greatest problem.

In time of drought people and animals die of starvation, not of thirst. The real shortage is of grass and browse for the animals and it is this fundamental need which dictates the lifestyle of the pastoralists.

When it does rain in northern Kenya plants and trees spring into life with astonishing rapidity. Tracts of stony desert that would appear incapable of sustaining life of any kind during a dry period will suddenly produce prolific grass; dull grey bush will become a vivid green; and in many places open ground will be magically carpeted with flowers. The overall effect of a few inches of rain in arid country can be as dramatic as a warm spring after a hard winter in more temperate climates.

But alas the season of new growth will be relatively short, forcing the nomads to move their herds as they look always for new browse and new grass, enquiring of any travellers what conditions prevail in other places and watching the horizons for

Previous page An aerial view of Poi in the Ndoto Mountains with a typical lugga (seasonal stream) draining into the Kaisut Desert

25

distant storms which might bring a brief fecundity a few days' march away.

Many desert dwellers will claim they can be on the move in two hours and sometimes the decision to travel will be made spontaneously. Once, when staying at Maikona on the edge of the Chalbi Desert, I saw a dramatic demonstration of the nomads' ability to be quite literally here today and gone tomorrow. It happened to be New Year's Eve and we sat out under the stars chatting to the missionary priest from Maikona, waiting to welcome the New Year at midnight, thinking of the millions of revellers in great cities across the world and savouring our own sense of tranquil isolation in the dark, empty desert, the nearest tarmac road 200 miles away. Above our heads the heavens glittered as only desert and mountain skies can; but far to the north a distant storm etched a blacker horizon with brilliant flickering light. Although too far away for us to hear the thunder, the lightning showed clearly the remote but towering clouds, their blue and violet shapes appearing with sudden flashes of clarity in the warm night air.

Next morning, an hour after dawn, Maikona lay as usual under a hard blue dome, the fierce sun already striking the parched bare ground. But everywhere the local Gabbra people were methodically packing their camels and by mid-morning the land was alive with caravans streaming north towards the site of last night's storm.

Although there are many differences between the social structures and customs of the varied tribes in northern Kenya, their inescapable necessity to be nomads in order to survive means they have much in common with each other. To me it seems inappropriate to emphasise the differences between, say the Turkana and the Rendille – and there are many – without first recognising that there really is a gulf separating the nomadic pastoralist from the settled tiller of the land; and an even wider one between the nomad and the city dweller. To emphasise this radical difference is, I think, rather more than underlining a platitude. Too many well-meaning schemes designed to improve standards of living in northern Kenya have come to grief because they are simply inappropriate in a nomad's world. The most glaring example of this is the way in which outsiders, be they missionaries, scientists or government servants, seem keen to make the nomads settle. Both subtle and obvious pressures are applied to persuade people to cease their wanderings. And yet if you want to live off semi-desert country by your own efforts, rather than by subsisting on free hand-outs of cheap food and aid, then it is necessary to be a nomad. Of course it may be possible to improve the nomadic way of life; but it is a fundamental mistake, in my opinion, to try to abolish the mobility of pastoral man which has been the single most important factor in his successful mastery of a very difficult environment.

The pastoralists' basic diet is milk, supplemented by meat and blood. Where it is possible to keep them cows are the most important stock; but in the harshest areas cows cannot survive, or give very little milk, and then the camel becomes the most

Stony desert strewn with lava boulders south of Mount Kulal. After rare rain, for a few astonishing weeks, new grass paints this land an amazing green; but for most of the year it is an arid waste

valuable beast in the herd. But for all the nomads sheep and goats are also important, being kept for their milk as well as their meat.

Recent studies have given accurate figures for milk production amongst the Rendille and Gabbra herds and so we know that an average camel will produce about 1.75 tons of milk a year. About a quarter of this will be used by the camel calf leaving an impressive 285 gallons for the owners. No wonder the camel is a revered animal which has symbolic as well as economic importance in desert communities. On average there are 1.4 camels to each member of the Rendille population, making over 400 gallons of milk available per person per year.

In addition goats and sheep each give about 20 gallons of milk per year. By keeping the kids away from their mothers except at milking time and then only letting them suckle from one udder the owners secure half the goats' milk for themselves; in the case of sheep the lambs are allowed to spend the night with the ewes so only a quarter is left for human consumption. However, in round figures there are twelve goats for each person so that well over 140 gallons are available from small stock for each member of the human population.

Calculations show that, in Rendille society, there is more than enough protein and energy in this daily diet of milk; a somewhat obvious conclusion, since the Rendille really do live on milk and could only do so if this diet supplied their every day needs. But the figures are important in giving an insight into the physical basis of the nomad's life; which is, quite simply, that if you have a gallon of milk a day you can survive in the desert. More importantly, they enable scientists to assess what margins of surplus the nomads have, whether they overstock their lands, and whether or not the energy demands their animals place upon the vegetation are a factor in creating desertification.

Meat, of course, garnishes the basic diet and animals will be slaughtered for feasts on special occasions as well as in times of drought and shortage. Nowadays some animals, especially sheep and goats, are sold for cash to buy luxuries like tea and sugar, blankets and maize. But most surplus animals are killed by the owners who benefit from the skins and leather as well as the meat.

Blood is the other traditional source of food. An arrow with a stop on it is shot at close range into the animal's jugular vein (it is usually a cow or a camel although the Turkana sometimes bleed goats and sheep as well). The blood is collected in a bowl and drunk neat or diluted with milk. All nomads believe blood gives them strength and will drink it in times of hardship or illness. Perhaps they are right; certainly blood is richer in protein than either meat or milk.

Here then we have the basic framework of the nomad's world: large herds of animals, kept mainly for their milk, which must be shepherded to make the best use of their arid lands. All their societies are constructed around this basic frame; but there are variations depending on the slight differences in rainfall – which may decide whether cows or camels are the best large animals – and on the origins and neighbours of the tribe.

All of them find that it pays to divide their herds, partially because the requirements of large and small stock are different, partially in order to utilise more land, and partially for the

Constant heating and cooling has split this twelve inch boulder into three pieces. Over millennia this mechanism turns stones into dust

Storms over Poi in the Ndoto Mountains, seen from the Kaisut Desert. Storms like this give a flush of new grass which can attract nomads from fifty miles away

convenience of elderly people and wives with young children who cannot travel so easily. Thus a common feature of nomadic life is the division of families and clans who may spend months without seeing each other. To remain cohesive in these circumstances a society needs firm rules and a clear set of customs to give the life of each individual some kind of structure.

Although there are wide variations between one tribe and another there are also many similarities: all of them have ceremonies which test a young man's physical courage before he becomes an adult; all insist that a child progresses through a series of roles in life moving gradually to the position of a mature adult; at each stage responsibilities and freedoms are clear and known, giving a sense of security in an uncertain world; all accord marriage great importance and welcome each new child: all encourage respect for other individuals, especially for the elders of the tribe; and, paradoxically considering their similarities, all tribes stress their differences (not to mention superiority!) to the other neighbouring tribes. Thus to an outsider, a non-pastoralist, there is a strong sense of similarity and we cannot help but observe that these peoples share common problems and a common heritage vastly different from our own. But for the pastoralists themselves the differences between one culture and another are crucial, in some circumstances even today becoming a matter of life and death.

To describe in detail each of the peoples in northern Kenya is beyond the scope of this book and is in any case a job for expert anthropologists. But in the following pages I hope to give an outline of the more striking characteristics of their traditional lives and some indication of the changes being brought by the modern world.

Turkana

A Turkana girl bailing water into a wooden trough in the bed of the Lokichar River. Amongst the Turkana everyone shares this chore; in some tribes it is a man's duty

Previous page A Turkana man and his herd of camels leaving Lake Turkana after drinking. This is the arid shoreline so graphically described by von Höhnel after his visit in 1888. Camels watered here must be marched into the hills to find good browse

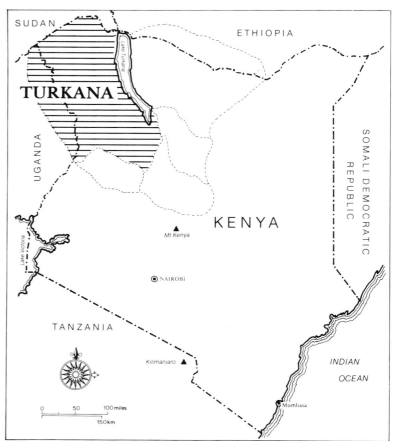

ALL THE PEOPLES of East Africa have been on the move for centuries so it always makes sense to ask 'where did these people come from?' But racial origins are obscure – in moving they have mixed and interbred – so anthropologists classify the different tribes by language, dividing them into four main groups: Bantu, Cushitic, Khoisan and Nilotic speakers. Of these the most numerous Bantu are agriculturists and the Khoisan are a tiny Bushmanoid group found only in Tanzania; so all the peoples in this book are classified as either Cushitic or Nilotic speakers.

Many first time visitors to Kenya underestimate the differences in language between one tribe and another, imagining that they are mere dialects. In fact the difference between, for example, the Turkana and Samburu languages is at least as great as between French and German; whereas the difference between Rendille and Pokot is something like that between Russian and English.

The Turkana are Nilotic people whose distant ancestors lived in what is now south-east Sudan. From here some moved into the Nile valley to become the western Nilotes. Others moved west and south, interbred with Cushites from the Horn of Africa, and became the ancestors of today's Paranilotes who comprise the well-known Maasai, the Karamajong of Uganda and the Kalenjin group of tribes who live mainly in Kenya's western highlands. The Turkana are part of the Karamajong group and moved into the plains west of Lake Turkana about 200 years ago. Since then they have expanded their territory, pressing back the Pokot and Samburu past the southern end of the lake and then advancing eastwards across the floor of the Rift towards Maralal and Baragoi. At around 220,000 they are currently the most numerous and probably the toughest of the pastoral tribes in northern Kenya. Certainly they occupy the most inhospitable land which includes – between Lodwar and the lake – the only area in East Africa with a rainfall of less than eight inches a year.

Being a tough people occupying a harsh landscape the Turkana have little time for moderation. Fiercely independent, proud to the point of arrogance, yet often happy and gay they inspire strong emotions; those who have worked amongst them either love or hate the Turkana and not infrequently do both!

They are the only pastoralists in northern Kenya who do not practise circumcision and so are despised by other groups who regard this as proof of inferiority; a feeling which the Turkana neatly re-direct upon their neighbours whom they equally despise for disfiguring themselves.

In utilising, nay exploiting, all the resources of their lands the Turkana have no equal. In several ways they have a kind of ruthless efficiency which enables them to squeeze more out of the countryside – and perhaps to cause more damage.

They keep all five species of domestic stock (camels, cows, donkeys, sheep and goats) and move constantly to find new browse and grass. A typical family will have four different herds and may move each of them up to 24 times a year to cover a total range of 8500 square miles. This kind of mobility needs an intimate knowledge of the countryside. They must know all the water-holes and which of them can be relied upon in really dry weather. And they must know not merely the best grazing and

A Turkana woman milking one of
her goats just after dawn. The
milk is collected in a hand-
carved wooden vessel whilst she
neatly traps the goat's kid under
her elbow; the kid's proximity to
its mother stimulates the flow of
milk

Two Turkana men with gourds
they have gathered in distant
mountains on the edge of the
desert. These gourds will be used
as water containers

38

browsing areas but which are best kept in reserve for use in a drought and which can safely be used during rare wet periods.

Important physical features of the landscape all have names; but to the pastoralist valleys and passes are more important than the mountain-peaks, so there may only be one name for a range of hills but individual names for each of its valleys and slopes. In this way Turkana can be precise in talking to each other about where they have been or where they are going; and they will question everyone they meet to assess the conditions in other areas. Since each of their five species has different needs it pays the Turkana to split the herds; whereas cows need grass, camels browse on bushes, so they use different areas. Sheep and goats make a third group and to a large extent donkeys can be allowed to fend for themselves. Perhaps this is because they are the only animals to have been domesticated in Africa, from the Arabian wild ass; the other animals have all been imported albeit some thousands of years ago.

Turkana, perhaps more than any other group, know how to get the most out of their stock. Although they use donkeys mainly as pack animals they will also kill and eat them in times of hardship; and whereas other nomads only bleed cows and camels the Turkana take blood from sheep and goats as well.

All pastoralists value sheep because they have more fat than goats – fat which can be mixed with ochre to decorate the skin, used to make leather more supple and rubbed into precious carved wooden vessels to stop them cracking in the sun, as well as being a luxury item on the menu! To increase the yield from their fat-tailed sheep, a unique breed which stores fat in its tail as a camel stores fat in its hump, the Turkana make an incision in the tail of live animals and remove fat for their own use. This operation is sometimes carried out on two separate occasions before the sheep is finally slaughtered; and although this may sound cruel, we should remember that the Turkana live in a cruel world and think of this as a useful aid to survival. Fashionable dog-owners have no such excuse for docking their puppies' tails!

Another trick the Turkana share with other pastoral tribes is to make their own dried milk by patiently flicking drops of milk on to a skin spread out on the ground in the hot sun. The resulting powder is collected in gourds and may be kept for months against the next dry season. When Turkana are on the move many of the bundles of gourds fastened to their donkeys will contain water; but others store the dried milk.

This is not to argue that all Turkana methods can be justified scientifically; like all nomads the Turkana tend to overstock their lands, having more regard for the number of animals than individual quality. Erroneously they think that in times of severe drought or disease large herds give them a better chance, since at least a few animals will survive. Scientists are unanimous in believing that if the pastoralists had smaller herds of better quality the available vegetation would be less severely grazed and in a bad drought less stock would die. But the traditional Turkana have no concept of land ownership and no doubt feel that if only one family reduces its stock the vegetation made available will be eaten by someone else's animals, leaving him with smaller herds and no gain.

Any time he feels thirsty a Turkana herdsboy can have a drink of milk!

Overleaf A young Turkana boy enjoys being with his father's herd

A young Turkana woman with part of her herd of camels

Goats leaving a Turkana homestead soon after dawn. The millet growing in the background will only produce grain in exceptionally good years

Right A Turkana woman carrying a gourd full of water. The smaller wooden container is used for milk

With all the travelling involved in looking after the herds a Turkana family will rarely be together; camels prefer the dry river beds where the trees stay green; cattle must be taken to grass and are herded by the younger men without families who can move on every day if necessary. In the dry season the cows must be taken into the mountains, sometimes for months at a time; but the Turkana will always say they live on the plains since this is what they prefer.

By driving the animals regularly to waterpoints and carrying gourds of water when they return, homesteads can be maintained up to seven or eight miles from a well. Water will be carried for small lambs and kids as well as for humans who can sometimes do without water for a period as they get enough moisture in their diet of milk. As everywhere in northern Kenya shortage of vegetation is the main difficulty which forces families to split and move on. This often means that a mother is separated from some of her children and from some of the stock allocated to her. In practice there is a lot of sharing of milk, meat and blood and the ownership of animals is only of real importance when making a gift, for example as bridewealth.

Sometimes, then, families may be separated for months; but usually they will all come together when it rains, in July, for a time of feasts and celebrations.

Although the Turkana do not practise circumcision there are other ways in which a young boy must prove himself before becoming an adult. At puberty two of his incisor teeth will be removed from the lower jaw and then later, at an initiation ceremony, he must spear an ox to prove his manhood to his elders.

Adult men decorate each other's hair in an elaborate coiffure of clay and carry with them everywhere a hand-carved neck stool so that they may sleep and rest without spoiling the hairdo. Any well-dressed man will also carry a spear and wear wrist and finger knives; both men and women wear lip-plugs and ear ornaments and, like all the desert tribes, decorate themselves with cicatrice markings.

Marriage is the most important event in life for the Turkana; although they practise polygamy (most men will have two wives by the time they are 40 and three when they are 50) adultery with other women is not tolerated and wives are regarded as the moral equal of the husband in informal relationships. As a symbol of the importance of marriage the bridegroom must give around fifty cows and camels and a hundred sheep and goats to the bride's family. Since this is about fourteen times the number of animals per head of population it is a tough assignment and involves the young man in much begging and borrowing from his relatives. Sometimes he will need to walk over a hundred miles to acquire a single animal. Although most of this bridewealth is given to the father of the bride some animals will go to her mother and to the other wives; and some will go to the father's and mother's brothers. So eventually the young man can look forward to receiving back much of the bridewealth, for example when his wife's sister gets married. In a sense the bridewealth is like a large downpayment on an insurance policy which brings returns in later life; after the marriage members of the bride's

A Turkana man with the traditional clay hairdo decorated with ostrich feathers

45

Turkana cattle: the horns of the bull are tied together to make them grow into a beautiful curve – rather like putting a brace on a girl's teeth!

A Turkana boy carrying a new-born lamb. Children start to look after the animals as soon as they can walk good distances

family owe obligations to the bridegroom, thus increasing his security. This makes him more independent of his own father and he will probably move away from his father's home as soon as he has enough animals to make this possible.

Independence is an ideal in Turkana society; and since it takes time, care and husbandry to build up a big herd the instant solution of stealing stock from neighbouring tribes is a popular one with all nomads.

All the pastoralists tell the same convenient fable to each new generation: that God gave all the cattle in the world to their own particular ancestors. So taking cows from neighbouring tribes is not stealing at all but merely recovering what is yours by right! Add to this philosophy that it is a status symbol to kill an enemy – for which distinction various decorations can be worn – and you will see that personal security is not one of the merits of pastoral life. Thus for generations the Turkana have been raiding the Pokot, the Samburu and Rendille tribes; and indeed they are not above a bit of raiding amongst themselves. Even in this aspect of their lives the Turkana seem to have adopted a ruthless efficiency and although many have been persuaded to give up raiding in recent years others have joined a new group of wandering brigands – the Ngoroko – who have modern arms from Uganda. Ranging far and wide this group of ruffians steal cattle from all and sundry with contemptuous ease. Then, when the Kenyan army are sent in to track them down, they vanish into the harshest, most rugged parts of the country where no four-wheel drive vehicle can follow and where soldiers bred in the cool highlands further south overheat in their camouflage battle-jackets and heavy boots.

Perhaps the Turkana's most hopeful quality is his total adaptability. In rare good seasons and in the very best areas of their arid lands they do try to grow some crops such as millet and a little maize. Unique amongst the pastoral tribes they have no objection to tilling the ground but rather turn their hand to anything and everything which will help to support them. Most pastoralists have taboos against eating the meat of wild animals and nearly all refuse to touch fish or birds but again the Turkana have no prejudice and will take advantage of anything which comes their way.

This makes them bad news for conservationists and it is no coincidence that there are no National Parks or Reserves in Turkana country. One professional wildlife man I know describes them as vacuum cleaners who eat everything that moves – and even some things which don't! I have talked to a young Turkana man who confirmed with pride that he had eaten lion and that it tasted good – and when I mentioned a catalogue of other animals he was only slightly doubtful about the wisdom of eating hyaena; everything else, including crocodile, was edible.

In the end one finishes up exasperated by the destructive side of the Turkana, but admiring them for their immense toughness; like some sort of crack SAS troops of the desert they seem to be able to tackle anything and go anywhere. Fearing nothing and no one they penetrate even the very harshest areas, finding sustenance in the most improbable ways.

And yet one fears for their future. In the past they have always

Above and overleaf A Turkana family migrating.
Children take turns to ride amongst the gourds –
some of which hold water and others the dried milk
which Turkana make by flicking drops on to a skin
in the hot sun. The rear donkey carries young
lambs and goat kids

been able to move on, each generation pushing back the frontiers
of Turkana land into new territory. Was this an essential feature
of their way of life, without which they must perish? Or can ways
be found to adapt them to modern Africa with its fixed frontiers
and border posts, without de-vitalising them? This, as we shall
see, is the conundrum for all the pastoralists.

Left Happy Turkana girls near Lokichar

Right Every Turkana man carries a neckstool to protect his clay hairdo when he rests. Each man carves his own stool – they often last a lifetime – and styles vary from one area to another. Some are almost identical to those found in Tutankhamen's tomb

Below A proud Turkana elder with ostrich feather in his clay headdress

Opposite A young Turkana mother with her baby

Left A young Turkana girl with the typical leather skirt at the door of her hut

Below, left Young Turkana children often go naked; but even half an hour after dawn – when this photograph was taken – the air is warm

Below The fat-tailed sheep is popular with desert dwellers as the fat from the large tail can be used as grease to salve their own skins, keep leather supple and prevent precious wooden vessels cracking, as well as being a source of food. The Turkana sometimes cut into the tail of a live sheep to remove some fat, an operation which enables them to double the yield from a single animal

55

Below For most of the year Turkana people dig for water in dry river beds. This is the Kosipirr River west of Lodwar

Bottom Turkana women carrying water home in the evening

Right Ostrich feathers are prized ornaments for Turkana women; the elder girl has a pendant made from ostrich shell

Pokot

Previous page During the dance celebrating the end of their three months' seclusion each circumcised Pokot boy carries his bow and arrows. As they sway their heads in time with the music, the bark cords give them a mysterious anonymity

Above The *sapana* dance over, these circumcised Pokot youths file off to feast on meat, cast away their seclusion masks and become accepted as adult men

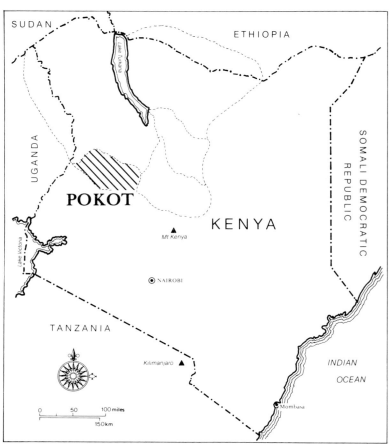

INSIDE THE THORN ENCLOSURE we were enveloped in sound. A hundred men stamped and chanted, torsos gleaming with oil and sweat, the rhythm of their bass voices bound together by beating drums. Above this deep, masculine sound a throng of dancing women sang an ululating descant, their bodies bobbing and swinging in the bright morning air; upraised arms wove a flickering pattern as they flourished cow horns laden with oil above their heads.

Adjacent to this group of happy, laughing dancers a mysterious chain of hooded figures swayed and stamped in time with the songs, their rope masks swinging back and forth in unison, giving them a faceless and powerful anonymity.

This was a rare and colourful *sapana* ceremony — only observed in seasons of plenty and the first for seven years in this area – to celebrate the ending of three months seclusion for newly qualified young men of the Pokot tribe. Twelve weeks previously these teenagers had braced themselves to endure with unflinching stoicism the most important event in their young lives – circumcision. Today, fully healed and initiated into the customs and lore of the tribe, they would become adult men, eligible for marriage.

Amongst the pastoral tribes of northern Kenya all but the Turkana symbolise the transition from childhood to maturity with this painful ritual; and in the agricultural groups further south circumcision is the rule not the exception. For the Pokot, Samburu, Rendille and Gabbra circumcision is the climax of a series of ceremonies and festivals which carry each individual from youth into maturity.

Although the details and forms of celebration vary from one group to another, for all these people circumcision is something awaited with excitement and longing as well as fear. 'It is a very hard custom,' said an educated Rendille friend of mine, now a qualified teacher. But he is in no doubt that his own children will follow ancestral tradition when they too come of age.

At the Pokot *sapana* ceremony, where I was a guest, the huge crowd throbbed with happiness. Men and women were adorned with ostrich feathers; mothers of the young graduates each had a special head-band sewn with cowrie shells and wore their brightest necklaces and ornaments. The young initiates, covered in skin cloaks, their faces hidden behind rope masks, each carried the bow and arrows they had used whilst hunting birds to prove their marksmanship. This is another common feature shared by many tribes; Samburu and Rendille also hunt birds during their initiation period, shooting with blunt arrows so that they must stun their prey in order to capture and kill them. Later the dried carcasses are made into a special headdress so that a young man may advertise his skill.

After perhaps two hours of happy dancing the young noviciates filed out of the fenced compound and went to rest under a group of trees. Here for the first time in several months they removed their hoods and masks in public and were given strips of meat by elders of the tribe. From now on they are entitled to wear the distinctive clay headdress which the Pokot have copied from the Turkana, sometimes mixing other people's hair with their own to make the style more impressive. To protect the *siolop* (rear of the

A Pokot girl

Young Pokot women bathing in the Muruny River, which rushes off the Cherangani hills on to the arid Lebatin plains. Throughout Kenya's desert regions the people will bathe whenever they are near water.

After circumcision and the *sapana* ceremony Pokot men wear a clay hairdo or *siolop*, painted to indicate their age-set. The diamond shape on the crown of the head (called *atoro*) often contains the hair of dead relatives

Opposite Skin capes and bark cords have hidden the faces of these boys for three months. At the *sapana* ceremony even their mothers have difficulty in recognising them

headdress) from damage they, like the Turkana, will always carry a small neckstool, so that even when they sleep their coiffure does not touch the ground.

Linguistically the Pokot are part of the Kalenjin group of tribes who live in the mountainous areas of western Kenya. Although they all have traditions of cattle herding most of these people have now settled as subsistence farmers and indeed two thirds of the Pokot themselves have settled in the Cherengani hills on the west side of the Rift Valley. Here, high on the slopes of these 11,000 foot peaks the Pokot constructed irrigation channels long before the first Europeans came to Kenya. Still in use today these ditches harness the mountain streams enabling the so-called Agricultural Pokot to grow a wide variety of crops and live in permanent settlements overlooking the wide plains to the north where their cousins the Pastoral Pokot still wander with their herds.

Perhaps it helps to place the nomad more accurately in an African perspective to know that the settled Pokot envy their wandering relatives on the plains, regarding them as rich – because of their large herds – and no doubt coveting the warmer desert climate in contrast to the cool mists of the mountains.

Being part of the Kalenjin group the Pokot are classed as Nilotic speakers: but this is a big group of languages and the Kalenjin come in the subdivision known as Southern (Highland) Paranilotes, whilst the Turkana are Karamajong Eastern Plains Nilotes. So although the Turkana and Pokot languages come from similar origins this means little more than classifying French, Italian and Spanish as Romance Languages. There is no more likelihood that a Pokot will be able to speak Turkana than that a Spaniard will be able to speak French.

In fact there is a lot of rivalry between the two tribes and for the Pastoral Pokot, hemmed in by mountains to the south, the Turkana are a constant threat. In spite of the government's efforts to stamp them out, cattle raids and killings remain a feature of Pokot life, exacerbated today by the use of modern weapons smuggled over the border from Uganda.

In spite of differences and rivalry with the Turkana, the Pokot have adopted many aspects of their neighbours' culture. Apart from the men's clay hairstyles and the neck-stools designed to preserve them, the use of lip-plugs, long narrow shields, wrist and finger knives are all similar to Turkana fashions. In a social sense there are close parallels too, for like the Turkana and Karamajong the Pokot people operate a complex age-set system through which each member of the tribe must pass on the way to adulthood, circumcision being only a part of this process, a kind of Pokot or Kalenjin addendum on a basically Turkana pattern.

Young women are also circumcised in Pokot society and they too go through a period of up to five months' seclusion whilst they heal and learn about the responsibilities of adult women. During this time they will paint their faces with ash, or a fine solution of mud, and wear long skin capes over their shoulders. This must be a difficult period in the life of a young woman. Apart from the pain of the operation and the time taken to heal there are other privations; isolated in a special hut she is now called a *chemirion* – no longer a girl but not yet a woman – and is allowed

to see neither father nor brother nor any other male relatives. Not allowed to speak she must tap with a stick to ask for food or water.

And yet, just as youths look forward to circumcision as the stepping stone to adult life, so a young girl past puberty will long for her initiation. Sometimes she may insist on being circumcised with a group of friends even though her parents feel she is too young.

There are often misconceptions amongst Europeans and other visitors to Africa regarding the circumcision ceremonies, especially as they affect women. It is hardly my place as a non-African male without medical training to make pronouncements on the advisability or otherwise of these traditional practices. But it does seem to me that no one should argue about these matters without recognising that both mothers and daughters desire to have the operation performed. Mothers may sometimes worry about the girl having it done too early; but they are in no doubt that it should be done.

In most tribes the operation consists of excising part of the clitoris; some groups also cut away a portion of the labia minora. This is normally done by an older woman who is known to be an expert and carries out the operation regularly. The young girls are expected to be brave and not flinch or cry out, although this is less important than for the boys who must give absolutely no sign of fear or suffering; otherwise they will bring disgrace on their families as well as upon themselves.

Anthropologists who have discussed circumcision with women of the pastoral tribes have been assured by married women of the Pokot and Rendille groups, for example, that sexual pleasures are not diminished by the operation. Amongst the Pokot, during the seclusion period immediately after circumcision, part of the training given by the older women is about sexual pleasure and they even assert that the cicatrice scarifications which they cut at this time add to the enjoyment of the sexual act.

But what is the positive value of such an arduous initiation? How do Africans benefit from the pain and suffering which they readily admit accompany this important period in their lives? Pastoralists I have talked to all emphasise the value of proving your manhood (or womanhood); of demonstrating in a clear, physical way your worthiness to be considered as an adult. Even amongst the well educated Christian sections of Kenya's population it has been estimated that as many as three-quarters of women and the vast majority of men still continue with the practice.

Are there parallels here with passing examinations in a modern society? Or with the popular veneration for high standards in athletic feats? Certainly in North America and western Europe society has respect for people who have survived an ordeal. The concept of heroism and the achievement of self-knowledge may act as a driving force on the rugby field, in the boxing ring or whilst climbing in the Himalayas. Specialist schools where young people are trained to pit themselves against the elements in the mountains and at sea are subsidised by many organisations in the belief that this type of tough experience is character-building. It seems to me there are some similarities here; and if we compare

A Pokot woman singing in the *sapana* ceremony which ends her son's three month seclusion period following his circumcision

African circumcision with features of other societies, in Asia for example, surely the parallels are obvious. Fasting, trials by burning, beds of nails and other tribulations are all designed for the participants to endure and surmount physical pain.

In his book *The Samburu* anthropologist Paul Spencer offers another hypothesis. Circumcision, he points out, marks a real change in the African's role in life involving new responsibilities and new patterns of behaviour. All the tensions which accompany the circumcision ceremony – and it is important to realise that the enormous psychological pressures on the initiate to be brave and not flinch or cry out are so effective that a young boy is more afraid of disgracing his family than he is of the actual operation – all these tensions, argues Spencer, create a kind of trauma, a form of shock after which it is much easier for the individual to believe that they really have changed and so accept their new role in life. This, suggests Spencer, is an important factor in achieving stability in pastoral society.

For myself I do not think we should look at circumcision in isolation. There are several other occasions when the desert people of northern Kenya inflict pain on themselves for what they consider to be good reasons. Piercing the earlobes to carry ornaments is an obvious example. Some pierce the lower lip and nose; all practise scarification sometimes creating an elaborate pattern of cicatrice markings on their chests and stomachs. All these habits involve pain; but young people will pester their parents to allow them to have the operations done just as a young European girl might argue with her parents in persuading them to let her use cosmetics. Of course all the desert people believe they look more beautiful after they have been treated in these traditional ways. One white anthropologist I know had to explain to pastoral people she was working with why she had never had her two bottom teeth removed – a habit which is common throughout northern Kenya, the teeth being levered out when a child is about fourteen, once again at the child's insistence. Clearly the nomadic tribes think adults look ugly if they still have all their teeth in the lower jaw!

Be that as it may, it seems to me that in the arduous desert country of the wandering pastoralists physical hardihood is not merely desirable: it is a pre-requisite of survival. Thus as a child develops he must pass a series of tests, each more difficult than the last, culminating in a trial involving his most intimate and sensitive parts. Enduring all this the new adult is ready to take up his (or her) role in life confident in his ability to meet all difficulties with fortitude. Childhood, in the desert, is a long lesson in acquiring relevant skills; herding and milking the animals; digging wells and baling water; building huts; travelling the lands; learning the tribal traditions and values. Circumcision is merely the passing-out parade, the graduation ceremony, the recognition that the time has come to take up adult roles. It is a complex matter and surely changes should be decided by the people themselves and not by outsiders whose pre-conceived ideas may have little relevance to the vastly different world of the nomad.

So many facets of the pastoral life are complex and intricate; it is anything but a simple lifestyle. Apart from the many physical

Opposite A young Pokot girl during the period of seclusion following her circumcision. During this time (which can be up to five months) initiates are not allowed to speak. They communicate by tapping with their sticks – for example to ask for food

The white clay on the girl's face is a symbol of uncleanliness whilst she heals, but the cicatrice marks on her stomach are a prized form of adornment

Overleaf Pokot women dancing and singing at the *sapana* ceremony celebrating the circumcision of their sons three months previously. The upraised horns contain oil for anointing people; hands and horns keep rhythm with the music

A Pokot man dressed for the *sapana* ceremony. His headdress is a kind of toupee, often worn by balding men

The traditional Pokot *siolop* hairdo is made by coating the hair with clay; friends help each other produce the desired effect using wood ash (or modern dyes) to colour the clay and an ostrich feather pompom for decoration

This Pokot elder also wears an ivory lip-plug and a pendant made from ostrich shell

A Red-billed Hornbill, a common bird of the dry
river beds in northern Kenya

Below A monitor lizard. Although harmless, many
people fear these lizards; the Rendille believe that a
goat bitten by a monitor will not give milk again

skills and the knowledge needed for survival there are a myriad of social *mores* to be observed and obeyed. Medicine, child birth, death, cattle rearing, eating, drinking, every aspect of life is governed by an interlocking system of traditions, superstitions and beliefs. Some are charming, like the Pokot idea that when a person dies they become a *Oryet*, a dust devil or whirlwind; when one rushes by they will try to guess who this might be. Other beliefs are frightening: if a Pokot man has killed an enemy then to propitiate an evil fate for himself, he must open up the stomach and cut away the heart; if possible he should chew a piece and then spit it out: afterwards he must purify himself by living in the bush wearing strips of uncured goatskin for a month before being re-named and having his arm marked with a scar (left arm for male enemies, right arm for females).

At a more trivial level there is a whole set of conventions regarding beads and necklaces. New-born babies wear beads made from the seeds of a creeper called *tilion* until they learn to walk; these are supposed to act as a charm against sickness and so are worn around the neck to prevent a sore throat and around the waist for stomach ache. Later an uncircumcised girl will wear a necklace made from the wood of a *kalkal* tree. Then, as soon as a young woman comes out of seclusion, she can start to wear a *soniok*, the characteristic bead necklace of Pokot adult women. There is even a convention about colours in Pokot society: red is a bad colour, yellow is associated with sickness, but green is good and blue – linked with the sky and rain – is best of all. Thus a woman whose child is ill may give away her red or yellow necklaces, hoping to get rid of the bad influences.

There are conventions too in men's attire, so that strangers meeting will quickly assess one another's status and position in society. If you find all this amusing think of conventions in more modern societies: white for weddings, black for funerals, top hat and tails for Ascot and a different kind of fashionable sports equipment for each type of game. Even the businessman, straightening his tie and clutching his smart, expensive briefcase, is motivated by the same desire to announce his position in the world as the Pokot warrior carving his first neckstool to protect his smart new hairdo. Wedding rings and good-luck charms, medallions of the Madonna and St Christopher, horse shoes and the number thirteen are just a few of the modern quirks and foibles not so dissimilar from the fashions and beliefs of the desert tribes.

Only after circumcision can Pokot women wear
these traditional *apedon* brass earrings. The lip plug
is made from the wood of a *muchukwa* tree and
the pendant is from ostrich shell. The woman's
heaped necklaces are typical of the pastoral Pokot

So bottle feeding is not a modern invention after
all! This Pokot woman is feeding her child with
goat's milk from a traditional gourd

77

Samburu

The magnificent horns of this bull are a prized status symbol. Using special ritual stones the first born son of each family may break a bull's skull and manipulate the horns to encourage them to form an elegant curve. Incredibly the animals survive, sometimes suffering more than one such operation

Previous page Two Samburu moran walking in the bed of the Uaso Ronkai, a seasonal stream south of Mount Nyiru

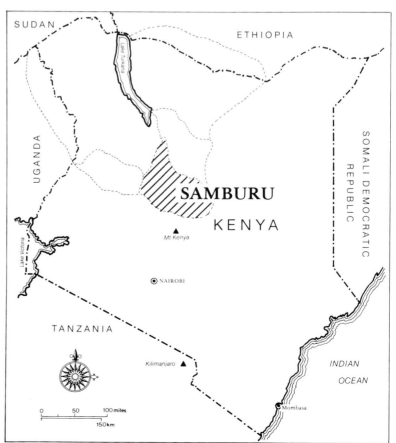

80

'WHY,' WE ASKED, 'have you decorated your cow? Is it special in some way? Does it give more milk, or was it born on the same day as yourself?'

'Only because we love our cows,' replied the youth, thinking our question strange.

We admired the animal, covered with neat blotches of mud arranged in symmetrical lines along its back and flanks. The boy scratched his cow, near the root of its tail, and they both stood patiently, enjoying each other's company, whilst I took photographs.

For the Samburu, cows are the centre of the world, giving milk, blood, meat, skins, hides, thongs, horns, ornaments, and status. Here a man's importance equals the number of his cows and life centres on their care and husbandry. To be sure there are also sheep and goats; but this is women's work. Men labour with their cows, water them, herd them, defend them against lions and will even sing about them. Sometimes they will go to great lengths to decorate them, marking their hides with long curving lines which are designed to enhance the animals, not merely indicate ownership.

In another amazing custom they will use special ritual stones to break the skull of a bull in order to manipulate the angle of its horns and so train them into a spectacular curve. This operation is sometimes repeated and astonishingly the animals survive and produce splendid heads, a kind of exhibition piece which is a status symbol for its owner. Another trick is to tie the horns with a cord which is tightened week by week, working like a brace on a child's teeth and making the horns follow a graceful line.

Of course this kind of practice is not confined to the Samburu; other pastoralists decorate their animals just as settled people will plant flowers to enhance a garden or city folk will add badges to their motor cars and fancy name plates to their doors. Sometimes the decorations may have another significance; when a Rendille girl wishes to make friends with a glamorous *moran* she may decorate one of his camels with mud patches thus encouraging him to invite her to a dance. But usually the meaning is simply as the young boy told us: 'because we love our cows'.

This concentration on cattle is an important factor regulating the Samburu way of life. Indeed a fascinating aspect of pastoral societies is the way in which variations in customs and behaviour correlate with the requirements and limitations of the animals they exploit. Thus the fact that cattle are the basis of Samburu life enables them to practise social customs – notably a higher rate of polygamy – that are impossible for their camel-based Rendille allies.

Only the relative lushness of their homelands enables the Samburu to concentrate on cows; this territory roughly forms a triangle with its base on the line joining Isiolo to Rumuruti in the south and its apex on Mount Kulal to the east of Lake Turkana in the north. Although this tract of country is all classed as arid land it contains many ranges of hills, making it easier to look after cattle since they can be taken to high pastures in a drought. In the northern part of their range the Samburu enjoy a close relationship with the Rendille people who, being camel specialists, utilise the dry plains without interfering with their Samburu

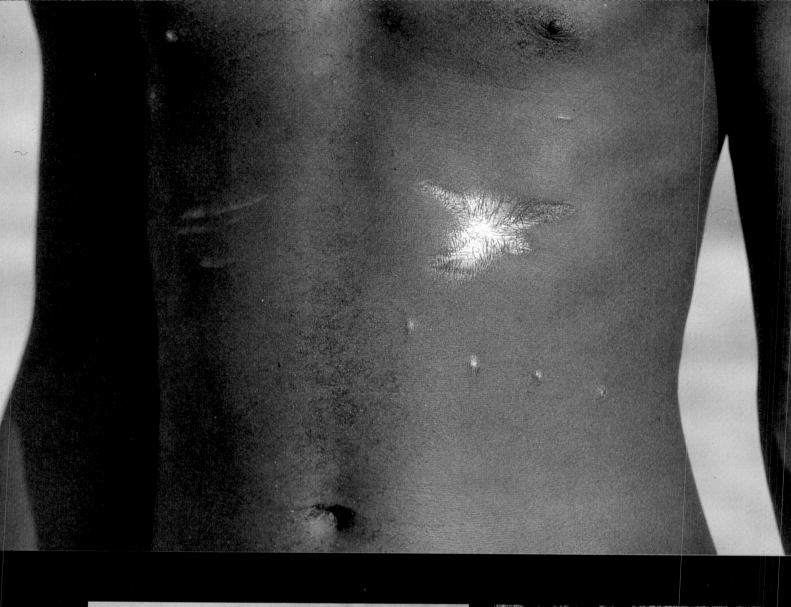

friends. The simple fact that cows eat grass whereas camels eat the leaves of bushes has encouraged these two peoples to forge close links – quite unlike the sometimes bitter rivalry between Turkana and Pokot, or between Turkana and Samburu.

Historians surmise that all the pastoral tribes once concentrated on cattle, like the Samburu of today. Archaeological evidence shows that camels have been spreading into Africa from the Horn for centuries – a symbol of increasing desertification. If this is so then the Samburu are an archetypal society, still able to live in the style which, perhaps, their allies and neighbours the Rendille used to enjoy before their lands became desiccated and they were forced to adopt the hardier but more difficult camels.

The long period of time which the young Samburu man spends as a *moran* or warrior, living outside the mainstream of society until he is over 30 years old, is quite impossible for the Rendille who need all their vigorous young men to look after the far ranging camels.

Not that his period as a *moran* is designed for the benefit and enjoyment of the young Samburu himsef: on the contrary, it is a social device which makes polygamy possible for the elders. As in other African societies the numbers of adult men and women are roughly equal; but since young women may marry as early as 15 and men must wait until they are 30 most elders are able to aquire two wives by the time they are 50. But structuring society in such a way that men are forced to wait many years before marrying is not easy and creates tensions. In Samburu society these tensions are controlled by an elaborate age-set system and a series of *ilmugit* ceremonies spread over a dozen years.

Casual observers are often struck by the glamorous side of a *moran*'s life; he is young, in his prime, elaborately decorated and can spend most of his time chasing the girls and planning pranks and adventures. But although this truly is one facet of the *moran*'s world there is another, darker side. He is cut off from the decision makers in the tribe – the elders – and must obey their rules; and whilst he is allowed to have love affairs he must not father any children and will often have to endure the frustration of losing girl-friends when they marry older men.

It is a measure of the powerful psychological forces harnessed to structure Samburu society that in spite of the constant thwarting of young men's desires and the relatively obsolete role of the warrior in modern Kenya the system seems remarkably durable; and what is more, in spite of the tensions such a system entails, the Samburu appear to be a very happy people.

The major cohesive force in all this seems to be the concept of respect, or *nkanyit*, which the Samburu must show to everyone, particularly the elders. This ideal of *nkanyit* is stressed throughout life as being the most valuable human quality; and it is a dominant theme during circumcision and the whole series of *ilmugit* ceremonies which follow. Reinforcing this positive virtue is the fear of being cursed, for any Samburu man has the power to curse another. The power of the imprecation depends upon the relationship between the one who utters it and the recipient, but firm belief in the power of such curses means they are very rarely used. The fear that they might be invoked is sufficient to persuade almost everyone to conform to the rules of Samburu society.

This Shankillah man carries a spectacular wound; but the four small marks below the wound indicate that he has killed an enemy

Left Samburu moran cutting up the carcass of a Grant's gazelle (see page 93)

Far left Samburu initiates, like their relative the Maasai, must shoot birds for their own headdress during the period of seclusion which follows their circumciscion. The birds must be shot with blunted arrows, which says a lot for the marksmanship of this young man!

Left A Samburu *moran* – member of the warrior class

Right No *moran* will move without his spear. Ivory earplugs and a long string of red and black beads also symbolise his status as a warrior and will not be worn by uncircumcised boys or older men

Below Cords made of wild sisal or bark are twisted into the real hair to lengthen the pigtail. One *moran* will help another to create this coiffure

Overleaf Crouched in a hole in the dry river bed, this Samburu married woman is filling gourds with water for her family. Her spectacular necklace is made from the fibres of palm leaves – although years ago they were made of hair from giraffes' tails

Right Common (or Grant's) zebra in Maralal Game Sanctuary

The Samburu are very tolerant of wildlife. Here cattle and zebra graze alongside each other within a few yards of a herdsboy on Maralal mountain

Another feature of Samburu life which may help explain their sunny disposition is the lack of tension between father and son. Each new age-set is created at a ceremony when a group of elders kindle a fire using the old method of twirling pieces of wood. These men become the fire-stick elders who are responsible for training and disciplining the new age-set through both circumcision and the long series of *ilmugit* ceremonies.

At any one time there may be living representatives of up to six or seven age-sets. Since there must always be at least three age-sets between a father and his son, whereas the fire-stick elders are always two age-sets older than the initiates, no father can be a fire-stick elder for his heir. In this way fathers are relieved of the worry and strain of disciplining their own sons; and it will be the duty of the fire-stick elders to make sure that the young men always show respect to their parents.

Very soon after the age-set has been 'kindled' the new initiates are circumcised at a public ceremony where, as with the Pokot, there is tremendous pressure on the young men not to wince or show any fear. Failure would be such a serious stigma on their families that the fear of flinching becomes more serious than the fear of pain. Added to all the singing and rhythmical chanting from the onlookers and elders, this tension creates an over-

powering occasion in the life of a young man emphasising his change in status. In the following month, whilst they heal, the youths shoot birds using bows and arrows which they prepared at the fire-stick ceremony. The arrows are tipped with latex which they gather from plants, usually in the mountains, and the birds they shoot are made into a headdress.

These headdresses and the bows and arrows are discarded about a month after circumcision during the first *ilmugit* ceremony which takes place, like all these feasts, at a special circular settlement laid out according to seniority. Each new *moran* must bring an ox to this '*ilmugit* of the arrows'. Two older *moran* will help him slaughter this ox and prepare and cook the meat. Then the *moran* must break one of the hip bones of his ox's carcass and give half to his mother whilst promising never to eat meat seen by a married woman.

This strange vow will bind him until he becomes an elder many years later; together with the privilege of being able to use red ochre to decorate himself it is one of the marks of being a *moran*.

At each ceremony the elders will spend time addressing the *moran* and lecturing them about their responsibilities and on the value of *nkanyit*; if the elders feel the *moran* are behaving badly they may arrange extra *ilmugits* to re-establish their influence. But most, like the first '*ilmugit* of the arrows', mark significant milestones in the *moran*'s progress towards elderhood. After five years at the '*ilmugit* of the name' he becomes a senior *moran* and is allowed to father children; but marriage is not allowed for several more years until the '*ilmugit* of the bull'. Even this is not the last of the series for there will be a final '*ilmugit* of the milk and leaves' when most of the age-set have married.

Then each *moran* is free to invite the elders to bless his family and can at last ignore the vows he made in the first *ilmugit* so

Above In all the nomadic tribes young men often help each other to adjust their appearance. Here a Samburu *moran* makes the final touches to his friend's hairstyle before setting off on a walk through the bush

Samburu goats on a boulder near Ngurunit

Opposite A young Samburu boy

A Samburu youth with his cow decorated with mud. The Rendille sometimes decorate their camels in the same way and young girls can invite the attentions of a *moran* by decorating one of his animals

many years before when he promised not to eat meat seen by a married woman.

Several other restrictions bind the behaviour of the *moran* and make him conscious of his special position. He cannot drink milk unless another *moran* is present and must never drink milk from the cattle of his mistress; he must not associate with married women; and he must not drink alcohol. Thus he is continuously reminded of his status in society; but at the same time he will look forward to the day when he will become an elder enjoying privilege and influence. The fact is that whether one agrees with the system or not it produces an ordered society which, because

Because of recent rain a mere scoop in the sand is enough for this Samburu *moran* to drink. Later in the season it will be necessary to dig much deeper

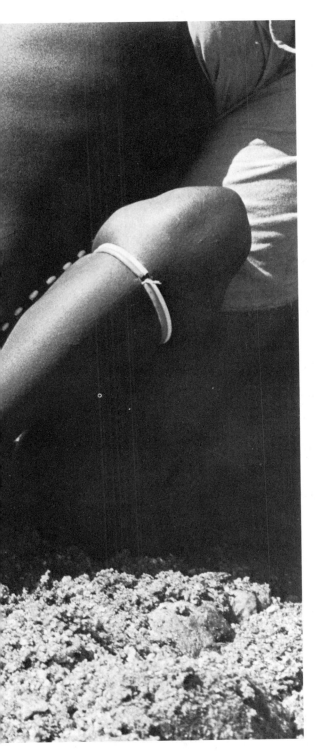

of its own internal disciplines, is more law-abiding in a modern sense than some other pastoral groups, notably the Turkana.

Some Samburu taboos have had very beneficial effects. Like many tribes they refuse to eat fish or birds and even today most Samburu will not keep chickens. An ex-professional hunter told me that on an early safari he gave his Samburu tracker a tasty guineafowl as a present and was surprised to find afterwards that it had been surreptitiously buried. Years later the tracker laughingly told the story against himself explaining how each evening as he returned to camp an uncovered foot of the hastily buried bird would catch his eye accusingly.

Like their Maasai cousins the Samburu have a taboo against eating the meat of wild animals and so wildlife is still prolific in their areas. The only animals which Samburu will consider eating are the ungulates like oryx and other gazelle which they regard as wild cattle; but even here there are inhibitions. Before licensed hunting was closed in Kenya a friend of mine had no difficulty in giving a Grant's gazelle to his Samburu trackers (page 82) who after skinning the carcass roasted and ate a quantity of meat. But they explained that adult men could not eat dikdik (a tiny antelope) and that although women and children could eat this meat they were not permitted to take it into the settlement but must eat it outside in the bush. It is perhaps 200 years since the Samburu and Maasai split up; now the Maasai live in southern Kenya and northern Tanzania and we find many famous sanctuaries in their territory. The Serengeti plains and Ngorongoro crater of Tanzania, the Maasai Mara National Reserve, Amboseli National Park and much of Tsavo West in Kenya are all in Maasai lands and contain the best concentrations of wildlife left in Africa.

Similarly in northern Kenya the wildlife sanctuaries are in Samburu areas. Perhaps the best known of these is the Samburu National Reserve on the northern bank of the Uaso Nyiru river. On the southern bank the Buffalo Springs National Reserve is administered by a different County Council but is ecologically part of the same area; and a few miles downstream the Shaba National Reserve is also in Samburu territory. Further north there is a small Game Sanctuary at Maralal, the administrative centre of Samburu district, where zebra and impala graze right up to the new houses on the edge of the town and you can see incredibly tame eland, Africa's largest antelope and usually a very shy animal, close to the verandah of the little lodge only a mile from the centre of Maralal town.

The number of animals to be seen in a reserve varies greatly depending on the season. After rain wildlife will disperse across vast areas but in a dry period the herds congregate where they can find water. At such times Samburu National Reserve can give spectacular game viewing with big herds of elephants as well as large numbers of zebra, impala, buffalo and oryx.

A generation ago wildlife was prolific throughout northern Kenya and all the pastoral tribes have lived in close proximity to wildlife for generations. Only in our own lifetime have the numbers been seriously depleted and alas in the last decade many species have been virtually exterminated over large tracts of country.

93

The Samburu have little fear of elephants and must often share a waterpoint with them in some districts. Traditionally they would only kill an elephant (with spears, of course) to prove their manhood. But high ivory prices and ruthless Somali traders turned many Samburu into poachers in the 1970s; so alas there are only a few areas in northern Kenya with elephants left today

Below Ahmed, the famous elephant of Marsabit, carried the finest ivory in Africa and was protected by Presidential decree; *Newsweek* reported his death (from natural causes) in 1974. But there are still some fine elephants on Marsabit mountain and the herds in Samburu National Reserve are increasing

Opposite The torso of a Samburu man; note the subtle cicatrice markings. Long strings of beads like these are only worn by *moran*

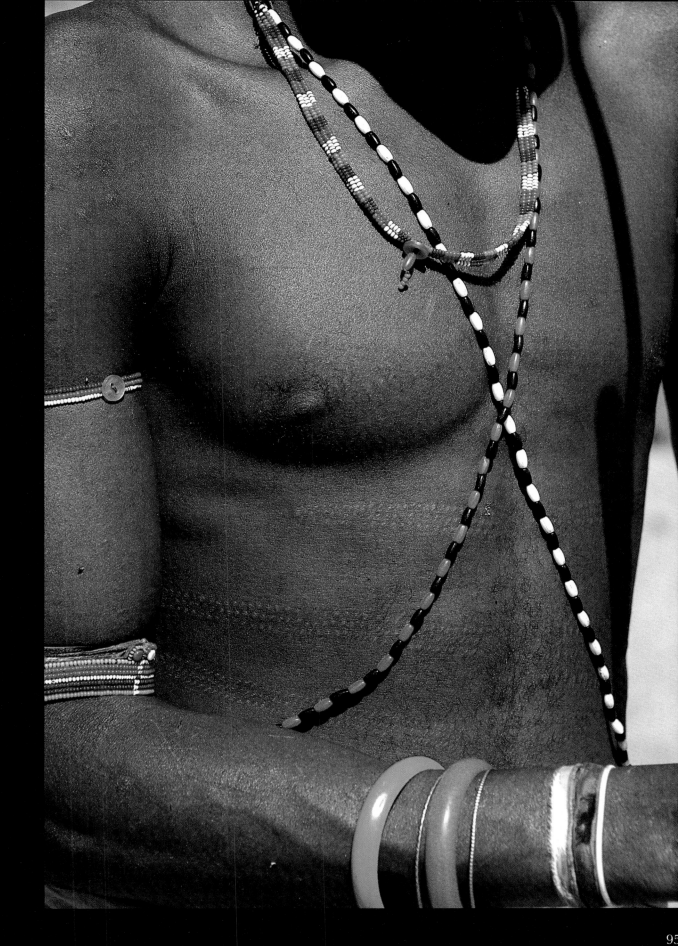

In the old days the Turkana and Pokot used rhino hide for shields; then, as they ran out of rhino, they turned to buffalo. Leopard skins were used as capes but these too are now very rare. Even the Samburu women's necklaces, which were made from the hair of giraffes' tails are now made of fibres from palm leaves. Elephant ivory was popular for lip-plugs, ear-rings and bracelets; and the Samburu who killed a lion would wear the mane as a headdress.

All Africans used to kill wildlife but although clearly some were more ruthless than others there was a kind of balance. In the last decades modern weapons and organised smuggling have increased the toll enormously, especially for elephant and rhino. Probably the worst ravages have been caused by the Turkana – who will eat any wild game – and the Somali who have organised an illegal trade in rhino horn and ivory, paying people like the Samburu, who would not normally have been interested in killing wild animals, to poach elephant and rhino for profit. Only ten years ago elephant were common around Mount Nyiro and the Ndoto mountains; but not today. Now you will find old skulls bleaching in the sun and when you mention these to missionaries they will tell you of a morning, maybe a decade ago, when travelling perhaps to Wamba they saw a caravan of men carrying ivory vanish down a lugga as the priest drove round the hill.

In spite of all this it is still possible to see quantities of game in northern Kenya, especially east of Lake Turkana and particularly in Samburu areas. Some of these creatures are exquisitely adapted to dry areas. Gerenuk, the long necked antelope, specialise in eating the leaves of acacia trees and can exist completely without water, obtaining enough moisture from the leaves. Beisa Oryx can be seen in the most inhospitable country north of the Chalbi Desert; they have an unusual metabolism which allows the body temperature to rise several degrees during the day and cool down again at night, thus avoiding the need to sweat and so conserving water: a trick which they share with the domestic camel.

The handsome Grevy's zebra, another dry country animal, even seems to be on the increase in the last few years since poaching has been brought under control. So distantly related to the common zebra that the chromosomes will not match and they cannot interbreed, Grevy's surprisingly can be mated with a domestic horse although the resulting 'zebroid' hybrids are themselves sterile, like mules.

Perhaps the most ubiquitous animals are Grant's gazelle which seem to thrive in the most unlikely areas. I have seen them in the Chalbi Desert, in the Suguta Valley and even on top of the Huri Hills – all waterless places.

Africans tell fables about many of these animals, often with a moral to emphasise traditional values. One of my favourites, told by many tribes including the Rendille, concerns the dikdik, a delightful little animal which is Africa's smallest antelope. Standing about 14 inches high and mating for life, each pair of dikdiks live in a fixed area which they defend against other dikdiks, marking their territory by painting twigs with a tar-like substance they exude from a gland below each eye. Tidy little animals, they always leave their droppings in one spot in their territory and after a few years this becomes quite a pile. (Black

Left This young Samburu girl has already started collecting beads from her boyfriends!

A young Samburu married woman wearing a spectacular necklace. Traditionally they are made from the hair of giraffes' tails but many women now have to make do with fibres from palm leaves. The necklaces are removed at night and hung above their husband's bed

This Samburu woman is on her way from South Horr to Mount Kulal – a distance of about 50 miles. She carries everything she possesses on the donkeys

Even in very dry periods the people of northern Kenya can find water by digging deep into the river beds. This Samburu woman is filling her gourds at Serolevi, north of Archer's Post

A Samburu woman making a clay cooking pot. She told me she had learnt the art of pottery from her grandmother and that there was no one else in the area who could do it. She bakes the pots in a charcoal fire and barters them for food and small stock – a rare example of indigenous trade

Lions are a constant hazard to domestic stock in northern Kenya. I put my own foot beside this pug mark within two yards of my tent after sleeping in the Samburu National Park, where lions are common, although they never molest humans. But throughout northern Kenya nomads lose between five and ten per cent of their stock to predators each year, and some people are injured or killed when trying to protect their animals

rhino do the same and make a bigger pile!) It is this dikdik latrine which is the subject of the legend. In the early days of the world it seems the dikdik was injured when he fell against an elephant dropping in the dark; so he called a meeting of the animals who all discussed the problem and agreed to be more considerate in future by leaving their droppings in a central pile. Alas! only the dikdik and his friend the rhino remember.

Other fables feature carnivores like the jackal, the lion and the hyaena which still menace the nomad's herds. All these predators still exist in considerable numbers in northern Kenya and are a constant source of concern to pastoralists. Hyaenas are the biggest worry but lions too are a hazard, usually killing out in the open in the day time but sometimes leaping into thorn enclosures at night. A recent (1980) study shows that up to ten per cent of domestic animals a year can be lost in this way, emphasising once again the rugged nature of life in the arid lands.

It is this kind of risk, the peril of having to face a lion when armed with a mere spear, which has created a need for the warrior class. No wonder the desert peoples have developed complex ceremonies and harsh tests which the *moran* must endure to prove his manhood.

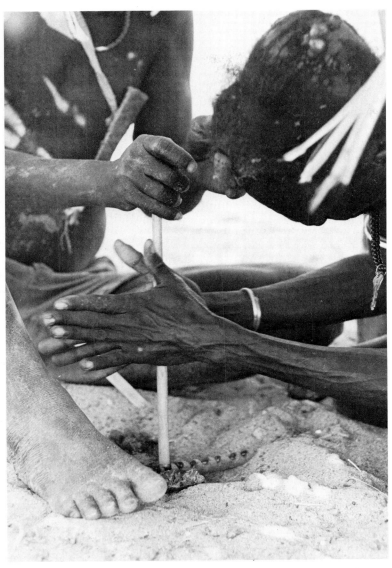

All of the desert tribes know how to make fire in this way. Only men perform this task and in many tribes it has a ritual significance. For the Samburu each age-set is created when a fire is kindled by the 'fire-stick elders'. Some men carry the kindling sticks as we might carry matches or a cigarette lighter, and can have a fire going in a matter of minutes

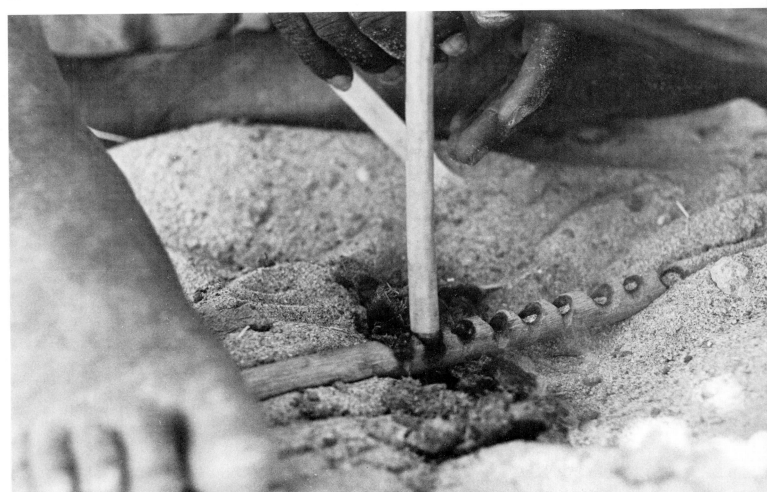

Dikdik is the smallest of the Africa antelopes, standing only fourteen inches high. It is well adapted to live in dry country where it is very territorial. Equipped with special glands at the sides of its face, it exudes a tar-like substance with which it marks bushes in its own area

Right A male gerenuk. These specialist dry country antelopes are adapted to eat dry bush and have hardly ever been seen to drink

The greater kudu is probably the most beautiful of Africa's antelopes. It is rare in Kenya but can be found on many of the mountains rising out of Kenya's northern deserts. Many tribes use the horns of greater kudu in their ceremonies

Left In the harsh world of the Chalbi Desert even the hyaena must succumb and become a feast for vultures

Left, below Beisa oryx in the Sibiloi National Park. They survive in many areas of northern Kenya. Their unusual metabolism allows their body temperature to fluctuate, thus reducing the need to perspire and so conserving moisture

The beautiful reticulated giraffe – only found in the northern half of Kenya – is not quite as tall as the more common Masai giraffe of southern Kenya. Often deep chocolate in colour, its hide yields a tough leather used to make buckets and sandals; so although it is now illegal to hunt in Kenya the giraffes are still subject to clandestine poaching

Grevy's zebra are also specialised dry country animals found only in northern Kenya. Larger and more handsome than the common zebra, they have narrower stripes which show a chevron pattern on both fore and hind quarters. Grevy's cannot interbreed with common zebra (the chromosomes don't match) but they have been crossed with domestic horses to form a hardy but sterile breed called zebroids

The endearing bushbaby has a prodigious ability to leap from branch to branch and occurs in many parts of northern Kenya, but being nocturnal it is rarely seen

Right A vervet monkey and her baby in Samburu National Reserve

Below An Egyptian vulture nesting in cliffs of volcanic tuff in the Sibiloi National Park

Right, below A white-headed vulture alighting on the carcass of a jackal

A male Somali ostrich: common in northern Kenya, the plumes of these magnificent birds are much used in head decorations by many of the nomadic tribes

Crocodile in the Uaso Nyiro River, which flows through Samburu country

Rodents, like this desert mouse, live in many waterless areas

Below Grant's gazelle are the most ubiquitous of the larger wild animals in northern Kenya. They can survive for long periods without water – presumably obtaining enough moisture from the vegetation – and I have seen them in the Chalbi Desert, on the Huri Hills and in the Suguta Valley, all waterless areas

Rendille

A herd of camels and goats being watered at the wells of Laisamis in the Kaisut Desert. Half a mile away, on the same day that this photograph was taken, free food from the United States was being given away at the Catholic mission; yet large herds like this cause overgrazing and desertification. Traditional inheritance customs mean that some pastoralists are rich while others who have lost their herds depend on aid

Previous page This Rendille village or *gob* is surrounded by frighteningly arid country. The tiny circle in the centre is the *Nabo*, a sacred place where elders meet, pray, discuss and make decisions. Women and animals do not go into the *Nabo* where a fire will burn day and night throughout the year.

The inner huts are for old women and newly weds. The different shades of grey indicate the corrals of the camels and goats – each with its miniature enclosure for young animals. A village like this could hold over a hundred people

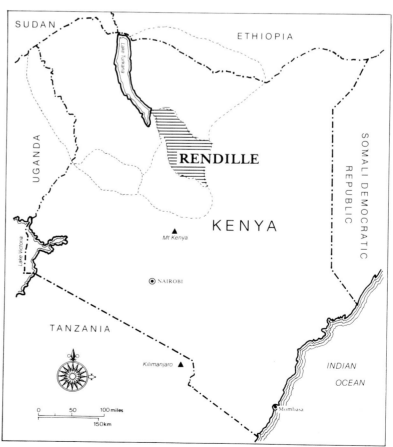

AROUND MIDNIGHT a new breeze rustled my sleeping bag; I turned over and found Orion the Hunter, a brilliant jewel at the centre of a glittering sky. Hours earlier we had watched the new moon's slender crescent chase the sunset over the horizon. Now, far out in the empty desert where there are no lights to dazzle the stargazer, the sparkling heavens filled my eyes.

A few feet away my friend Gambare stirred on his camel skin.

'What do your people call the Milky Way?' I asked.

'It is the path where the hyaena dragged his mother,' he replied. 'That animal is so cruel he even beat his mother.'

I pointed out Orion and Gambare explained that for the Rendille the three stars we call the belt are two men stealing a goat. In the inverted tropical sky the Great Nebula, which for Europeans is the sword hanging from the belt, becomes the upraised stick of the last man beating the central goat, whilst other nearby stars are the owners chasing after the thieves.

Shooting stars, Gambare told me, are a bad omen; so if you see one you must say 'fall with peace'.

That night I was sleeping at the settlement, or *gob*, of Gambare's family to see the ceremony of *hai* which is celebrated every month at the new moon.

In the late evening, after the new moon had been sighted, Gambare's father burned fragments of fragrant wood and leaves inside his hut, caught the fumes in a hand-made milk container and carried them to his forehead. Then he drew a piece of ivory through the perfumed smoke column before rubbing this too on his torso and forehead. Gambare and I were then treated in the same way whilst all the time his father chanted incantations which, I found later, express gratitude for the month which has passed and ask for rain and peace in the next. The wood burnt in this ceremony comes from the forests on Mount Marsabit; a few fragments kept in a special pouch will last for many moons and the ivory is kept secretly as a personal charm.

Squatting in the low-roofed hut, under the camel skins and the hand-woven sisal mats made by Gambare's mother from wild sisal which grows in the hills, I was struck by the quiet dignity of this little ceremony. Each family in the *gob* celebrated that evening, some performing the ritual just outside their homes.

Afterwards Iltirim, Gambare's father, marked our foreheads with a creamy paste of ghee and red ochre to show we had observed the *hai* custom. Later in the evening, as Gambare arranged his camel skin and my son and I adjusted our camp beds outside under the stars, I could hear gentle talk in subdued voices coming from the nearby huts; there was a warm sense of the little community desiring only peace and rain.

In the first grey light before dawn Gambare's mother awoke us as she broke sticks and blew on the embers of last night's fire. Soon we drank hot tea, prepared as a luxury for the foreign guests, whilst Venus hung, huge and brilliant, low in the eastern sky. Minutes later the brightening disc threw shafts of light between the clustered huts and suddenly the whole settlement was bustling. Goats were milked and led out for the day's grazing by young girls wearing, on this special morning, *aharusete* marks of chalk on their faces, to show they too had celebrated *hai*.

The loose red and white necklace this young wife is wearing is the equivalent of a wedding ring. Exceptionally, after many months of quarrels, a wife might return this necklace to her husband if she wanted to refuse him. Only young or unmarried women wear the metal ornament on the forehead. The small cicatrice markings below this woman's breast are for decoration whilst the larger ones are supposedly medicinal

Rendille camels about to move off to a new site. Castrated male camels (*folas siban*) or sterile females (*mahan*) are used for this work

Overleaf Rendille settlements at Korr, dominated by the distant Ndoto Mountains

Worn only by Rendille
child is a son, this uniq
called a *doko*. The mot
style until the baby is w

Right A Rendille baby g
mother's hut

Gourds and containers
has its own name and s
right the first and third
unusual for a woman to
every married woman
marriage by either hers
from roots, they last fo
will drink from it and it
occasions. The second
both called *madhal* and
Below the left hand *ma*
sandals for the unborn
have. The metal anklets
also used in ceremonies
To the right is a new
which grows on Mount
Finally, to the far right, i
symbollically on the hu
behind the necklace, in
used in the blessing of t

Gambare's mother had a final duty; donning her special *oko*, a skirt made from goatskin decorated with cowrie shells, she stepped outside the settlement and gathered stones. These she placed in two long lines, again to denote that the ritual of *hai* had been carried out. People will not step over these stones but will go round them out of respect for the tradition; and when the settlement moves the tell-tale lines remain, a token of the months spent here.

The monthly *hai* ceremony is the simplest of several festivals observed by the Rendille people. Following the rains, when there is plenty of browse and grass, all the young people and stock join the elders' settlements to celebrate *soriu*. Camels provided by each family for the feast are killed in a special order according to the status of their owners. As each beast is slaughtered the blood is painted on to the other camels and splashed on to sheep and goats as a kind of blessing whilst the elders use staves to dab themselves.

The use of blood, which is so common amongst pastoralists, both as a food and as an anointment, often worries westerners. Too much nonsense about Dracula and too many loaded words such as 'bloodthirsty' make blood taboo for us just as birds are taboo to the Rendille. For the nomads blood is no more nor less than one of their three most valuable foods; milk is also used in important ceremonies – like *almhato* which marks the beginning of a new year – and meat is a feature of them all. In Lancashire pigs' blood, made into black-pudding, is still regarded as a delicacy and although I cannot think of a ceremonial use for real blood in Europe surely communion wine is a symbol for the same.

Sometimes, it seems to me, there are uncanny parallels between old European customs and those of the African nomads. In Italy rice is still thrown at weddings, anointing, as it were, the bride and groom with an important form of food – surely the same in principle as the use of blood or ghee by the desert tribes.

The ceremony of the firestick elders, which begins a new age-set for Samburu men, reminds me of the flame carried from Olympia for the beginning of each new Olympic Games: and the continuous flame kept alive on so many altars and memorials has a striking similarity to the fire which burns for 24 hours a day throughout the year in the sacred *nabo* at the centre of each Rendille settlement. Women and children are not allowed into this small circle fenced with thorns; it is where the elders meet to talk over problems and the affairs of their families and clans. Only in the annual *almhato* festival can women and children enter this holy place, pouring milk into a special container which is blessed by the elders. This complex ceremony used to take over two weeks but nowadays many settlements carry out the important rites in two or three days. The elders shave their heads and wear decorations made from ewe-skin. When the head-bands are prepared the sheep's hooves are left attached to the skin and form part of the headdress which each man will keep for many years to be worn on special occasions like *almhato*.

During the ceremony two fires are lit just outside the settlement and all the people and stock walk in procession between

Young Rendille girls often help to look after baby brothers and sisters

Left Living on aid from a Catholic mission, this Rendille woman has allowed her hair to become long and unkempt, her clothing dirty. Other Rendille, still living in a traditional way, regard her as a drop-out from their society and despise her appearance

This lovely young woman is from a clan mid-way between the Rendille and the Gabbra, but she has recently married into a Rendille family. The fibres of her necklace are made from palm leaves

This man is carving a milk container or *soror* from the solid wood of a tree the Rendille call *hagar* (acacia). When he has finished the wooden base, his wife will weave the bottom out of roots, seal it with blood and charcoal and smoke the inside to sterilise it

As soon as they can walk Rendille girls start to help with the family goats

Opposite, above The morning after the new moon this mother dons her *oko* skirt and places stones in line to show that her family celebrated *hai*

Opposite A Rendille man proudly exhibits his cicatrice markings and neatly excised navel. In an operation unique to the Rendille, a boy's father will make a series of tiny cuts around the navel when a boy is about eight years old. If the operation is done badly the navel protrudes and is called a *bajo* – a derisive insult. But a neat successful result is a source of pride. No self-respecting Rendille girl would agree to marry a man with a *bajo*

these fires. A kudu horn, called an *arap*, is blown for this procession, the horn being another precious possession which is used for many years. Finally the elders visit each hut in the settlement and, after anointing themselves with ghee, go inside to chant prayers asking for rain and peace. When I attended *almhato* at Gambare's *gob* I was once again impressed by the dignity of this last blessing, the quiet rhythmical chanting, the etiquette of entering and leaving each dwelling in order of seniority, every man resting his stave at the entrance and collecting it again as he left.

After the ceremony was over all the elders sat in a group outside the settlement, still wearing their ewe-skin head-bands, chatting quietly to each other as though savouring the atmosphere of tranquillity they had invoked.

Living mid-way between the Samburu and Gabbra tribes the Rendille share cultural traits with each. Their periodic festivals like *soriu* and *almhato* are very similar to those of the Gabbra and it is from the Gabbra that the Rendille have copied the special white hat called *dhub* which certain influential elders are invited to wear as a public honour. But the Rendille circumcision ceremonies resemble those of the Samburu and indeed the Rendille synchronise their own cycle to follow two years after the Samburu – a scheme they have followed for over 150 years.

Traditionally the Rendille should gather on the shores of Lake Turkana a year after a new age-set has been circumcised for an enormous ceremony called *Galgulumi* when all the new warriors bathe in the lake. *Galgulumi* used to last several days and included much singing and dancing as well as several rituals performed by the young men. But in 1981 the ceremony was carried out at Lake Paradise, a small crater lake on Mount Marsabit, with a mere fifty young men representing all the other *moran*. 1981 was a very dry year so it was impossible for the Rendille to move to Lake Turkana as they would have done in the old days and indeed according to tradition the ceremony would not have taken place until 1986. But nowadays the Kenyan Government is encouraging the desert tribes to speed up their ceremonies so that the *moran* can settle down at an earlier age, thus reducing raiding and stock theft.

Whether this proves to be a change for the better remains to be seen. Certainly the old Rendille ways forced each young man to be a *moran* for many years and delayed his marriage often until he was over thirty years old. But this was an important factor in reducing population growth as well as making young men available for life in the camel camps where they would tend the main herds. Like the Gabbra, their northern neighbours, the Rendille concentrate on camels for their large stock, a decision enforced by their extremely arid lands, for camels have major advantages over cows in really dry country. But they are also more difficult to keep and so Rendille and Gabbra societies are structured to take account of this.

For example camels can cover much greater distances – up to forty miles a day is possible, whereas ten is good going for a cow – and can do without water for much longer periods. Cows must drink at least every three days but camels can manage for ten

days in dry weather and indefinitely after rain when green vegetation will satisfy their moisture requirements. Camels also give more milk, three to four times as much as a cow during the year, so there is little doubt which is the better animal in dry country.

But to get the most out of camels their herders must be able to cover the same huge distances and take them into waterless areas where camels can browse on vegetation the cows would never reach. Sometimes the owners subsist for weeks on the milk of their animals without extra water.

This tough work is done by the young Rendille *moran*; the camel herd is taken away from the main family leaving only enough animals to sustain the older people and young children. The *moran* thus has a heavy responsibility compared with his Samburu counterpart and so he is less isolated from the mainstream of society; and although the marriage of Rendille men is delayed by their own age-set system it seems to be for a different purpose. For the Samburu, delaying the marriage of young men makes polygamy possible for the elders; but monogamy is the norm in Rendille society and the delayed marriage may be important in preventing population growth which cannot be sustained in a camel economy.

Since it is relatively easy to increase herds of cows the Samburu feel they can support an increasing population – erroneously, since the land which supports the cows is not growing, but that is another matter. Camel herds, however, are very difficult to build up, not only because camels have a long period of gestation and lengthy intervals between calves but also because there are heavy losses due to disease; in a bad year up to 45% of young camel calves may be lost and even in good years camel pox and tick infections kill many animals. So the Rendille know they cannot afford large families and manage things accordingly.

Rendille camels are always milked by men who usually work in pairs grabbing two teats each; if one person tries to tackle this job the two spare teats rise up into the udder and do not drop down again for some time. In many ways managing camels is an intricate business and needs much skill. Most males are castrated, to reduce fighting, so it is important to choose the best bull, called *orr*, which wears a hand-carved wooden bell and a decoration made from seeds by the girlfriend of the *moran* who looks after the bull. But the Rendille, like other desert peoples, live with disaster looking over their shoulders; a long drought or epidemic may wipe out many of their animals and they cannot afford to invest all the reproductive capacity of their herds in one bull, however promising. So they hedge their bets by practising hemi-castration on a few other male camels; this apparently quietens them sufficiently to stop them fighting but leaves them capable of mating if the chosen bull should die.

The castrated males, or *dufam*, are slaughtered in a drought or on very special occasions and some are trained to carry loads and fetch water. This is one of the few jobs Rendille women are expected to do with camels; the animals driven by women have a special name – *hal* – and can carry up to 30 gallons of water, enough to last a family for many days.

Thus the hardy camel which imposes greater burdens on

Opposite The black necklace and brass earrings show that this Rendille woman is married. Already a grandmother, she is popular in the village for her sense of humour

A Rendille woman preparing a goat skin which will be used to make clothing

Previous page The New Year ceremony of *almhato* over, these Rendille elders relax and enjoy the feeling of tranquillity they have invoked

Left Wearing the ewe skin headband to celebrate *almhato* this old Rendille man checks the arrows given him years before by a Samburu friend. Rendille don't normally use bows and arrows, so these are the equivalent of an exotic souvenir

This old Rendille man anoints himself with ghee as part of the festival

Rendille men makes life relatively easy for women. Samburu wives are expected to help with milking cows and must struggle with small donkeys when moving house or collecting water; only a few gallons can be carried by a donkey and so more frequent visits to the water points are needed. Camels can also carry far bigger loads when families migrate so that all in all Rendille women are better off and have a higher status in society expressed perhaps in the elaborate Rendille marriage ceremonies which can last eight days.

Competition is different in these two societies; in the Samburu world, where polygamy is the aim of every elder, wives are in short supply and so, in addition to the bridewealth, the bride's family will expect to receive other gifts in later years. But for the Rendille there is a fixed bridewealth of eight camels; once these have been paid there will be no further pestering which must be another factor in creating a dignified relationship.

When a Rendille wife has a first born son she may wear a *doko* hairstyle, an elaborate crest built up with clay which is the most spectacular woman's coiffure worn in northern Kenya and another symbol of the women's better position in Rendille families.

Linguistically the Rendille and Samburu are poles apart: the Samburu are Nilotic and the Rendille Cushitic speakers. But for generations they have been allies and there is much intermarriage. The Samburu desire for wives means that Rendille girls are always in demand and this interchange is fostered by the so-called Ariaal Rendille whom the Samburu call Masagera. Living in the land between the two main tribes, from Laisamis across the Ndoto mountains towards South Horr, they have a kind of intermediate society whose customs have Rendille origins but are modified by Samburu influences. Most Ariaal are bi-lingual and this tribe provides a route for men and women to migrate out of Rendille society into the Samburu. Whereas the Samburu desire for extra wives motivates the movement of women towards the Ariaal, pressures of a different kind act on some Rendille men. Since it is so difficult to build up camel herds the Rendille tradition is for the first son to inherit the whole herd, leaving his brothers with only a small number of animals. By trading with the Ariaal these less favoured heirs may be able to exchange goats and sheep for camels – something they could never do with the Rendille proper – and so make contacts which can lead to some of them moving into the alternative society.

But although some individuals do leave Rendille society, like other nomads they are proud of their own traditions and tend to look down on their neighbours. Once again I am struck by parallels in western societies: in Europe, for example, the Swiss tend to look down upon their Italian neighbours, regarding them as a disorganised, untidy people who lack discipline. The Italians in turn contemn the Swiss, thinking of them as closed and unfriendly, being too controlled and lacking any real history.

To assist them in maintaining their self-esteem peoples everywhere emphasise the often minuscule differences between their neighbours and themselves; in this way the Rendille have preserved their language and their identity even though they number less than 20,000. One cannot help admiring their tenacity in

A Rendille blacksmith fashions an aluminium bracelet whilst his wife pumps air into the charcoal fire using bellows made from goat skins

Right All Rendille women learn how to cure skins and make them into garments. This skin is being sun dried; later it will have oils rubbed into it to make it supple

Rendille call this ancient game *bola*. Played over vast areas of Africa it is a game for men only

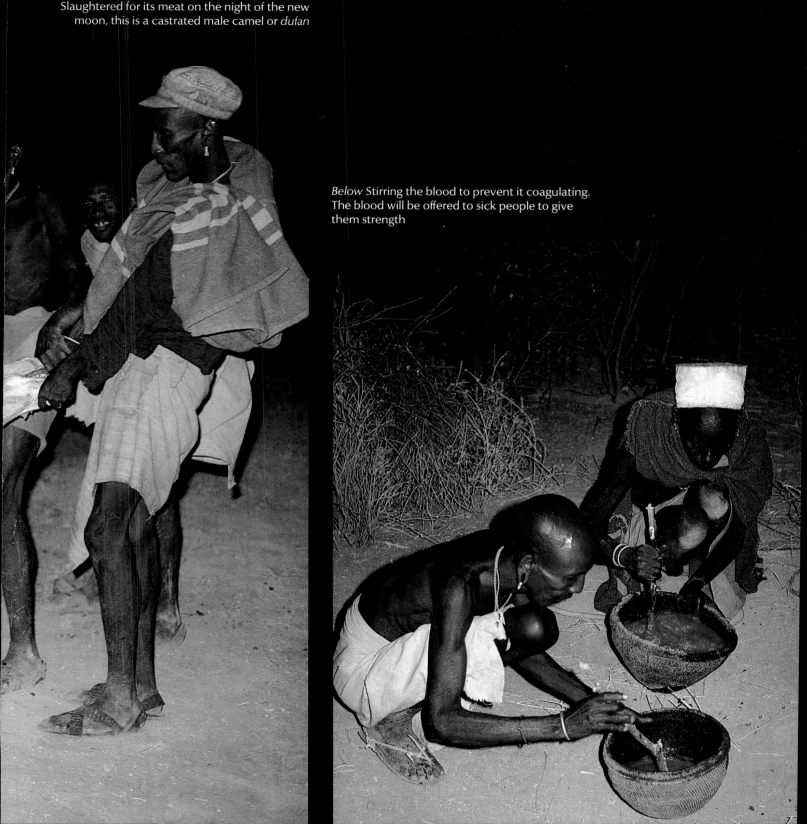

Slaughtered for its meat on the night of the new moon, this is a castrated male camel or *dufan*

Below Stirring the blood to prevent it coagulating. The blood will be offered to sick people to give them strength

This Rendille man's unusual necklace can only be worn by those who have killed an enemy – a sort of Military Cross for valour. He told me that he had killed a Samburu *moran* who was trying to steal his goats near the Ndoto Mountains. The Rendille are widely respected as fierce defenders of their stock and traditionally castrate any men they kill, returning home with the gruesome spoils as evidence of their prowess

A Rendille elder blowing an *arap* made from the horn of a greater kudu – rare antelopes which still survive in the hills of northern Kenya. Used on ceremonial occasions, such horns are treasured and may last several generations

This mat, called *ilal*, is made from the branches of palm trees secured with thongs of camel hide. Each Rendille woman makes one as part of her dowry and it is used as a bed with bush underneath and skins on top. It is also used as a natal couch; the young child in the photograph was born on this *ilal*

preserving their structured, ordered society whose only permanence is the handing down of oral traditions from one generation to the next. Whether the modern world can offer something to improve the Rendille way of life or will instead merely disrupt their intricate and finely balanced society is a question hanging over all the desert nomads which will be discussed in the final chapter of this book.

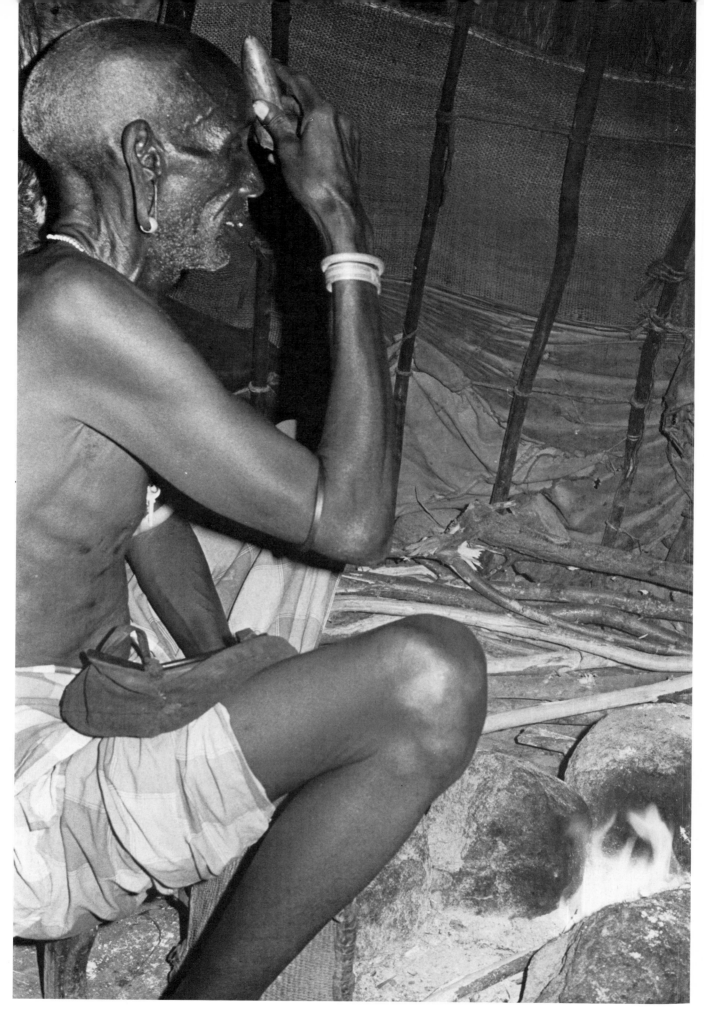

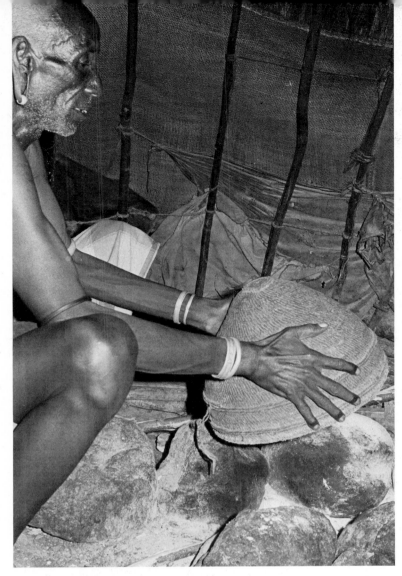

Opposite Iltirim, a Rendille elder, rubs his head with a sacred piece of ivory after passing it through the smoke from burning fragrant wood as part of the *hai* celebrations following the sighting of a new moon

Left After collecting the scented smoke, Iltirim carries the basket to his forehead and immerses his face in the fumes

This man is celebrating *hai* outside his house. He carries smoke from a tiny fire between his feet up towards his face

Left A Rendille *jijo* – a design copied from the Gabbra – is made by every bride before she gets married and is used by the husband for drinking milk. Woven from root fibres it is coated with blood and charcoal to keep it watertight and will last for twenty years. Cowrie shells are used as decorations by many tribes and are thought to be a symbol of fertility

Milk and grass are placed in this hand-carved wooden trough as symbols of plenty during the Rendille ceremony of *almhato* to celebrate the New Year

Gabbra

This 'Gabbra bidet' is used by women after childbirth and whilst menstruating. Sitting astride the framework they burn aromatic herbs underneath the basket to fumigate themselves

Previous page A distant thunderstorm seen from Maikona in the Chalbi Desert. Next day hundreds of people were on the move hoping to find new browse created by the storm. According to Gabbra legend, thunder is caused by drum beats in the sky; long ago a young girl sitting on a dried lion skin was carried aloft by a whirlwind. Even today the frightened girl still beats the drum-like skin and we hear claps of thunder

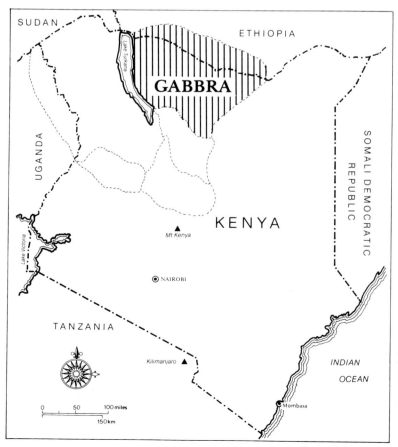

FROM MAIKONA we drove south. Leaving the mission and cluttered huts below us we climbed a barren rock-strewn valley dotted with stunted trees. 'Turn left now,' said the boy, eyes shining, proud of his English and thrilled to ride in the white man's car.

Away from the track we bumped up a stony rise and paused. From here the land slopes down to the north, huge, wild and open. There is no soil; only stones and then more stones. Here and there a few lines of tufted grass accentuate the vast perspectives; a mile away a gully with a bank of black lava scores a dark line across the empty plain; beyond this other gullies, other stones stretch and stretch to a far horizon notched with the blue cones of the distant Huri Hills.

'There!' pointed our guide. 'It is the village of two houses.' Two domes, like halves of coconuts, roped to the ground; a few thorny branches to form a fence; human figures. We trundled down the slope, our wheels crunching the stones, and parked just short of the settlement. As we walked over the boy called out greetings in his own language and at the huts we shook hands whilst the boy explained. 'They are friends of the Father. They want to meet Gabbra people, perhaps to take photographs.' We offered tobacco, some tea and sugar. A series of questions, the boy answering for us; the two men of the settlement, discussing with each other, their wives standing near and listening. Then the older man addressed our guide. 'It is all right,' he translated and there were smiles all round; we shook hands again and the women came shyly to touch my son's blond curls.

Over the next few days we visited 'the village of two houses' each morning and evening so that I was able to photograph these Gabbra people in their everyday life. As has happened so often, with all the pastoralists I have seen in northern Kenya, the presence of my own wife and children helped in making human contacts and creating trust in spite of the language difficulties so that these Gabbra people relaxed and overcame their fear of *buda*, the evil eye.

Amongst the Gabbra there is a widespread belief that some people possess the power of the 'evil eye', bringing misfortune to other people and animals simply by looking at them. This leads to a strong mistrust of the camera and many Gabbra people refuse to be photographed; so personal introductions from someone known and trusted are invaluable.

At the village of two houses the senior man had become a Catholic and the word of the missionary priest was more than enough to ensure goodwill with him. He wore a white cylindrical hat or *dubo* typical of the *Dabela*, senior Gabbra men who have a special position in the tribe being responsible for many of the important ceremonies.

Like many other tribes the Gabbra have an age-set system, their word for an age-set being *luba*. They are part of the Galla group of Eastern Cushites, the first peoples to move south from the Horn of Africa, so like other Cushites they practise circumcision for both men and women. But amongst the Gabbra circumcision is not the most important festival in life; true each adolescent must be circumcised, but the important ceremonies come later as each *luba* moves to another position in society.

145

Made to last a lifetime this five gallon Gabbra water container is woven from the roots of local plants and decorated with cowrie shells. First split into long fibres and then boiled, the roots are woven so tightly that the container remains waterproof for many years. Blood is smeared on the inside and fat or ghee on the outside to stop the fibres breaking

After circumcision there are four classes for adult men in Gabbra society. These are called *Kommicha*, *Yuba*, *Dabela* and *Jarsa*; each *luba* or age-set moves up this scale along with all the other members of his *luba* thus creating an inevitable pattern in the life of each individual. Each of the four classes had its own place in society; the *Kommicha* are relatively young men who are still learning about the tribal traditions and their responsibilities. They are allowed to marry and start their families but it is the more senior class of *Yuba* who make decisions and effectively govern the tribe. After several years as *Yuba* the whole age-set will be promoted to the third class called *Dabela* when they will wear the distinctive white *dubo* hats and will play important roles in the ceremonial life of the tribe as well as being consulted by the new *Yuba* who now carry the practical responsibility. Still later the *Dabela* will retire to the fourth class of *Jarsa*, old men who still exert influence by advising their juniors.

The biggest festival in Gabbra life, called *Jila Galana*, marks the transition from one class to another. At this festival the newly circumcised youths become members of the new *luba* or age-set which will carry them through life. They acquire the status of *Kommicha*, while the present *Kommicha* become *Yuba*, the *Yuba* become *Dabela* and the *Dabela* retire to become *Jarsa*. At the same festival the new young *Kommicha* choose two representatives called *hayu* who become important officials in the tribe, called on to solve difficult disputes.

Although held together by its unity of language and tradition the Gabbra tribe is divided into five sections or *gosa*. Each of these has a sacred village or *yaa* where their important ceremonies and rituals take place. In a sense the *yaa* is the capital of the *gosa*; the horns and drums used during ceremonies are kept in the *yaa* and the inhabitants are always made welcome when they visit other settlements where they are offered gifts as well as hospitality.

Thus each individual Gabbra man will be a member of a particular *gosa* and he will go to the *yaa* of that *gosa* for all his important ceremonies. It will be at this *yaa* that he will become a *Kommicha* and later move through the stages of *Yuba*, *Dabela* and *Jarsa* as he matures and grows old. Only very rarely will the five *gosa* meet at a ceremony called *Korra* when long-standing disputes will be discussed and settled. *Korra* was last held in 1934 and although it was planned for 1981 the rains that year were poor and so it was once more postponed.

Although almost 80% of Gabbra people live in Kenya they have strong connections with Ethiopia and many of their *yaa* are either close to the border or actually in Ethiopia. One section – called Galbo – go to Mount Forole on the border north of the Huri Hills for their festivals whilst the Odola group celebrate at Turbi near the Marsabit-Moyale road.

Amongst the nomadic wanderers of northern Kenya the Gabbra keep a more accurate calendar than anyone else and apart from the important festivals which mark the passage of each age-set from one class to another there are other rites which celebrate the months and years. Only their more settled neighbours the Boran are more respected for their accuracy in measuring time.

In the Gabbra method a new day begins at sunset, so that one

Each adult Gabbra man will carve his own stool like this

This Gabbra milk container has symbolic as well as practical uses. Made by either the bride or her mother before a wedding, it is an essential part of every home and will be used by the husband for drinking milk

day is the period between one sunset and the next – a simple and logical system in a land close to the equator where the time of sunset varies very little throughout the year. Like us the Gabbra count days in groups of seven – which they call *torban* – with a name for each day of the week. Each new moon, or *baati*, is celebrated with a ritual and the Gabbra use the same word *jia* for both a month and for the moon. They have different names for each of twelve lunar months which follow on in an infinite cycle; but for the Gabbra there is no relationship between months and years which are counted quite independently. This seems strange to us until we remember that in modern calendars the twelve months have been made to fit into a year by adding days arbitrarily so that they no longer have anything to do with the cycles of the moon. To the Gabbra, living in a land without artificial light, the moon's cycles are of great practical importance and it is interesting to note that their important festivals are held on the ninth, tenth and fourteenth days of the lunar month when there will be good moonlight; weddings and sacrifices to remember the dead are held on the third and fifth days after the full moon when people can sing and dance or merely talk in the moonlight.

Like the Rendille the Gabbra celebrate each new moon, burning incense and marking themselves with chalk. The Rendille festival is modelled on that of the Gabbra who also give the lead in celebrating the beginning of each new year with their *Almado* festival (*Almhato* for the Rendille) which takes a total of 15 days.

For the Gabbra there are 365 days in a year; they take no account of leap years and so their traditional *Almado* festivals are not in step with modern calendars. Quite how the Gabbra and Boran have adopted this system is not known although it seems likely they derived it from Arabia; certain words used for measuring time may have Arab origins. But the Gabbra ability to reckon their calendar is impressive in their non-literate nomadic world. Since there is always one day left over after the 52 whole weeks in a year of 365 days, each new year begins on a different day of the week and thus the Gabbra count years as the Monday-year, the Tuesday-year and so on. Over a long period a major event will be used to define more clearly the Wednesday-year of the drought, or the Thursday-year of the dead sun (for an eclipse). This system of counting years means they are in cycles of seven and it is this cycle which determines the big festivals of *Jila Galana* when the age-sets move on from class to class. The gaps between one *Jila Galana* and another are always a multiple of seven years; this century it has been held in 1909, 1923, 1951 and 1972. Seven years is too small an interval and would result in men in their prime having to retire and become *Jarsa* and another important factor is that each man's sons must be two classes below him. By having gaps of 14, 21 or even 28 years between one *Jila Galana* and the next the Gabbra ensure that men do not retire into the *Jarsa* class until they are really old. But each individual looks forward to going through the full cycle giving those who survive into old age a sense of completeness since they occupy each role their society has to offer.

This sense of completeness, of experiencing the whole of life,

147

applies to their material culture as well as the structure of society, for Gabbra people, like the other desert tribes, traditionally make all their own artefacts. Carved wooden troughs, wooden camel bells, buckets made from giraffe hide, water containers woven from the roots of certain trees, stools, combs, pouches, gourds, all are the responsibility of the individual who must collect the materials and work them in traditional ways.

The only expert artisans in the pastoral societies of northern Kenya are the blacksmiths (with here and there a very few potters). In all the nomadic tribes the smith occupies a special place in society being simultaneously respected and despised. Unable to marry the daughters of ordinary men they form a sort of sub-tribe of their own, passing on their skill from one generation to the next, so that it would be difficult for the son of a blacksmith to become a 'normal' member of society. Even if he

Gabbra goat herds in the open bush seen from Dabandabli, a volcanic hill on the northern edge of the Chalbi Desert

gave up the art of forging and acquired a herd of animals so that he could live like his neighbours it would be several generations before his offspring could intermarry freely.

Just why the blacksmith should be denigrated is something of a mystery for his skill is both essential and decorative as he forges spears, knives and more harmless jewellery. But most pastoralists would regard the smith's work as both dirty and arduous and they are generally believed to have the ability to curse people, usually in association with iron which, being used in circumcision operations as well as in dangerous weapons, is a substance with almost mystical properties. Perhaps it is the blacksmith's odd blend of skill and power linked to menial work which creates the ambivalent feelings all pastoralists have towards their only traditional specialists.

For ordinary Gabbra people the hardest physical labour is watering their animals and here there are two differences between the Gabbra and most other groups in northern Kenya caused by the geology of their area. The Samburu and Turkana, for example, find most of their water in dry river beds. Although the people must dig for water during most months these sand luggas are always lined with acacia trees which can remain green almost throughout the year, nourished by the moisture underground. Only towards the end of long dry periods do these water points fail and then the Samburu and Turkana people take to the cooler hills where there are night mists and occasional showers and so more green vegetation.

On the high peaks which stud the desert plains, such as Kulal, Mount Nyiru and the Ndoto mountains, it is still possible to find a tinkling stream long after the rivers on the plains have dried up; so the mountains provide the dry season grazing. But in Gabbra country, instead of dramatic granite peaks we find the softer volcanic cones of Mount Marsabit and the Huri Hills.

Rising to over 4,000 feet and over 50 miles long the Huri Hills are a range of cinder cones totally without surface water. Here rainfall soaks straight into the ground, through the porous volcanic ash, until it reaches impervious subterraneous rocks which carry the water far out into the desert where it emerges in permanent springs at places like Maikona, Kalacha and North Horr.

Thus geology imposes an inverted pattern on the Gabbra who must take to the hills immediately after rain when the green flush of vegetation gives their animals enough moisture to survive and the owners can live on the plenteous milk. Then after a few weeks of luxury, as the green turns again to brown, the Gabbra must retreat to the plains and make use of their permanent springs, wandering ever further for the sparse grazing and browse between each visit to the wells.

In dry months, such as January and February, there can be huge congregations of camels and goats at these wells and it may take many hours to water a big herd. But once again there is no shortage of water, at least by the standards of the nomads themselves. For the Gabbra, as for the other wanderers of Kenya's north, the real shortage is of grazing and of browse.

Tragically all the efforts of outsiders to offer help to the Gabbra pastoralists have failed to touch this central problem.

A Gabbra woman leading her family's camels to a new home-site. Under the curved sticks, which will make the framework of their homes, one of the camels carries a pregnant woman whilst the milking herds will be far ahead led by the men

Overleaf Two Gabbra youths guarding their camels at a waterhole near Kalacha on the edge of the Chalbi Desert

This old Gabbra woman has just crossed the Chalbi Desert with her camel

More wells and more water, schools and churches, hospitals and dispensaries have all been provided at several important foci for the Gabbra people; but while many of these measures have alleviated suffering and opened new doors to some individuals the productivity of the land has remained at best unchanged and in some places has been much reduced because of the concentration of stock around the centres which causes irreversible damage to the fragile vegetation.

Some of the harshest country in northern Kenya is inhabited by the Gabbra whose homelands include the inhospitable Chalbi Desert, a huge dried out lake bed which still floods after heavy storms but for the rest of the year is a baking pan of sterile saline soils. Parts of the Chalbi are coated with salt, its pure white crystalline texture an uncanny counterfeit of fresh clean snow. Some Gabbra gather this salt and sell it in the markets further south at Marsabit; but apart from this the Chalbi is a useless tract

Right A big herd of Gabbra camels leaving the wells at North Horr in the Chalbi Desert

A Gabbra family migrating and apparently wading through a mirage caused by the shimmering heat

of country, merely a harsh barrier to be crossed by long chains of loaded camels, the curved poles of the portable Gabbra dwellings nodding like huge strutting birds. Seen from a distance these camel trains wade through shimmering mirages, towed above their flickering reflections by human silhouettes, the very epitome of desert wanderers.

Whereas the modern traveller can thrill to the huge spaces of the Chalbi, humming across the firm sands in a four-wheel drive vehicle, choosing a line at will and revelling in roadless freedom, it is a different story on foot when one feels pinned to a board, creeping across the sun-scorched sand with stoic stamina. Even the more productive areas of Gabbra country have a frightening isolation and one cannot help but admire the style in which they inhabit this unyielding land. To me they are the aristocrats of northern Kenya, both men and women being often beautiful.

Unique amongst the nomadic tribes Gabbra women wear their hair long in attractive ringlets. Metal bracelets and necklaces are common and mothers advertise their status by wearing a double string of metal beads (usually aluminium) on the crown of the head. Traditionally silver was a prized ornament and there are still a few Gabbra women wearing large silver coins as pendants. In the past the Gabbra have obtained these coins from Ethiopia, but nowadays they are extremely rare, most having been sold in times of drought.

It is not clear whether there has been any significant change in the climate of northern Kenya in our own lifetime; but several features of Gabbra country clearly show the gradual desiccation which has been going on here for many aeons. Apart from the Chalbi Desert itself, with its dried out lake bed and shifting sand dunes, there is the parched hinterland of Lake Turkana, now the Sibiloi National Park which contains probably the richest fossil site in Africa.

Geological evidence shows that Lake Turkana has been drying out for at least six million years. Sediments laid down by the shrinking lake, along with layers of volcanic ash or tuff, have preserved the fossils which prove that this area was once more prolific in plant and animal life than the best of Kenya's wildlife sanctuaries today.

Even modern Sibiloi National Park contains a surprising amount of wildlife. Reticulated giraffe, beisa oryx, Grevy's and Burchell's zebra, tiang (a topi-like antelope) and Grant's gazelle are all common here. Amongst the predators lion, cheetah, golden jackel and hyaena are fairly easy to find and hippos wallow in the lake. One forte of this area is its large crocodile population which live mainly on fish at the summit of a food chain based on algae which thrive in the mildly alkaline waters of Lake Turkana.

But although the protection of wildlife was one justification for the creation of the Sibiloi National Park the preservation of extensive fossil sites was another and perhaps more important motive. It seems incredible that on the shores of the world's largest alkaline lake, which contains the world's largest fresh-water fish (Nile perch grow to over 300 pounds!) and perhaps the world's largest crocodile population, we should also find the continent's most important fossil site; but this is indeed the case.

In Kenya no one is allowed to live, or graze their animals, inside a National Park and so the creation of Sibiloi National Park (originally named East Rudolf) in 1970 excluded the Gabbra people from over 600 square miles of traditional dry season grazing grounds. But this was done after negotiations involving Gabbra elders who were happy at the choice of the name Sibiloi, after the mountain on the Park's southern boundary.

Koobi Fora – the famous fossil site – is also a Gabbra name meaning 'the hill of the shepherd's camp'. (*Fora* is the word the Gabbra use for the camp where young men look after herds of camels which have been taken away from the villages to find good browse, the equivalent of the Maasai *manyatta* in southern Kenya.) Discovered in 1967 by Richard Leakey, now director of the National Museums of Kenya, Koobi Fora has proved to be not merely very rich in fossils but also very large. It is possible to find specimens along an isochronous line seventy miles long, giving scientists the chance to collect whole communities of prehistoric animals and so piece together a more complete picture of past habitats. Modern techniques are so refined that even individual fossilised grains of pollen can be examined and identified with electron microscopes and incredible numbers of bone fragments have been found. Thus we know that instead of the 95 species of mammals we can find in Kenya's best modern reserves there were at least 160 in Sibiloi two million years ago. This impressive total included three different kinds of hippopotamus, three types of giraffe and three species of human! These last three are *Australopithecus* – an excellent specimen was found by Leakey himself in 1968; *Homo habilis* – the famous 1470 skull of 1972; and *Homo erectus* found in 1975.

There is still some controversy amongst anthropologists regarding the 1470 *Homo habilis* skull, dated at 2.4 million years, which Leakey and his team regard as being on the direct line which leads to *Homo erectus* and ourselves. But the *Homo erectus* skull of 1975 is of much less controversial significance since it is identical in form to other *Homo erectus* skulls found in Peking and Java. The Koobi Fora specimen is much older, thus providing evidence that early man may have originated in Africa and migrated out into Asia much later.

One of the strengths of the nomadic tribes is their clever use of local materials; this Gabbra woman is weaving a roof mat from wild sisal found on hills at the edge of the desert

Women are responsible for building and maintaining the huts; these sisal roof mats last for many years and are easy to carry when a family migrates

The 'village of two houses', isolated in the barren wastes of the stony desert near Maikona

Two beautiful Gabbra women photographed near the foot of the Huri Hills in northern Kenya

This little Gabbra boy is wearing a bell as a precaution in case he wanders from home. Rendille children wear bells on their ankles for the same reason

Using a scaffolding of wooden poles, a team of men and women lift water in giraffe hide buckets from a deep well on Marsabit Mountain

Opposite Young Gabbra men of the Kommicha class bale water into hand carved wooden troughs. Fed by springs from the Huri Hills over thirty miles away, these Gamura wells are an important oasis in the Chalbi Desert

Of course this does not prove that mankind has his origins in Gabbra country but instead emphasises what a magnificent fossil site this is. No doubt other *Homo erectus* skulls will be found elsewhere in Africa; but there are few places where fossils come to hand as readily as they do at Koobi Fora. 30 miles inland the complete skeleton of an elephant has been unearthed whilst another 30 miles to the south a huge petrified forest has been dated at over 20 million years.

These unimaginably ancient fossils form a fitting climax to a journey in northern Kenya. 400 miles from the nearest tarmac road, an overland trip to Koobi Fora involves several days travelling through pristine semi-desert country with many glimpses of the traditional, almost pre-biblical ways of life of the Samburu, Rendille and Gabbra peoples. There is a sense of achieving a view-point in time, of the cluttered twentieth century dropping away and wider perspectives opening up, so that we see ourselves as having only recently settled in our concrete world.

But at Koobi Fora even the nomads whose timeless lifestyles may already have survived a few thousand years are suddenly seen as modern men. Here, in the gullies below boulder-strewn ridges, ordinary layman's eyes can find a dozen fossil fragments in as many minutes and one is forced to confront the appalling gulf of pre-history. Stepping back down the hill of time we find the pastoralists our near neighbours, only a few yards away on the summit slopes; but at the fossil sites time becomes a cliff where we must look into the void and try to grasp the fact that for over twenty thousand centuries – for that is what 2.4 million years means – our ancestors have roamed these slowly desiccating shores.

Returning from the immense perspectives of pre-history one wonders at the frenetic rush of modern life and the often destructive influences which the twentieth century exerts on traditional societies. Too many well-meaning people have done harm in northern Kenya, making it harder instead of easier for the pastoralists to survive.

Must the nomads become yet another extinct way of life? Or can they continue with their wanderings and perhaps even survive some cataclysmic extinction of the modern world?

Right The fossilised tooth of a pig from Koobi Fora. Millions of years ago, when there were almost twice as many species of mammal as there are today, there were four separate genera of pigs in this habitat

Opposite These petrified logs of an old cedar-like forest in the Sibiloi National Park have been dated at 26,000,000 years. Now this once lush land is arid semi-desert

Below Dated at about 1,500,000 years old, this marvellously preserved skeleton of an elephant has tusks which are large by modern standards. Now on view in a roofed shelter, it is about twenty miles inland from Koobi Fora

Right Occasional thunderstorms carve deep valleys in the fossil-bearing sediments near Koobi Fora. On these slopes it is easy to find ancient bones

Opposite Weaving is an important part of a woman's life in the desert. Baskets, roof mats and water containers are all made in this way and every woman is expected to make her own

Common salt in the Chalbi Desert where Gabbra people gather the snow-like crust to sell in markets at Marsabit and further south

Loading their camels with huts and possessions in the early morning, these Gabbra women are preparing to migrate. Experts at travelling light, they can be on the move a few hours after dawn

Top left Even the slightest shower will trigger plant life in the desert. Flowers like this Desert Rose (*Adenium obesum*) bloom and many creatures benefit from new growth

Above Hibiscus vitifolius: these lovely flowers are often found at the edge of montane forests in northern Kenya. This one was photographed on Mount Kulal

Left Tribulus cistoides: preferring sandy soils in the warm semi-desert plains, these perennial plants produce a carpet of yellow flowers after rare showers of rain

Right A Gabbra man

Left Camel bones in the Chalbi Desert. About 45 per cent of the Gabbra herds die before they are two years old

Right Camels loaded with water at the wells of North Horr

Below A typical Gabbra camel loaded for migration. The tall sticks will become the framework of the hut; the rolled mat at the side of the camel is used to make a bed when covered with skins and also serves as a natal couch. If necessary, old people, pregnant women or small children will ride on the camel under the awning

A spitting cobra. Although very rarely seen – for all snakes are timid – these reptiles are common in northern Kenya. Some Gabbra *gosa* believe that they have a mystical relationship with snakes and put out drinks of milk for them. One group uses snakes in some of its rituals

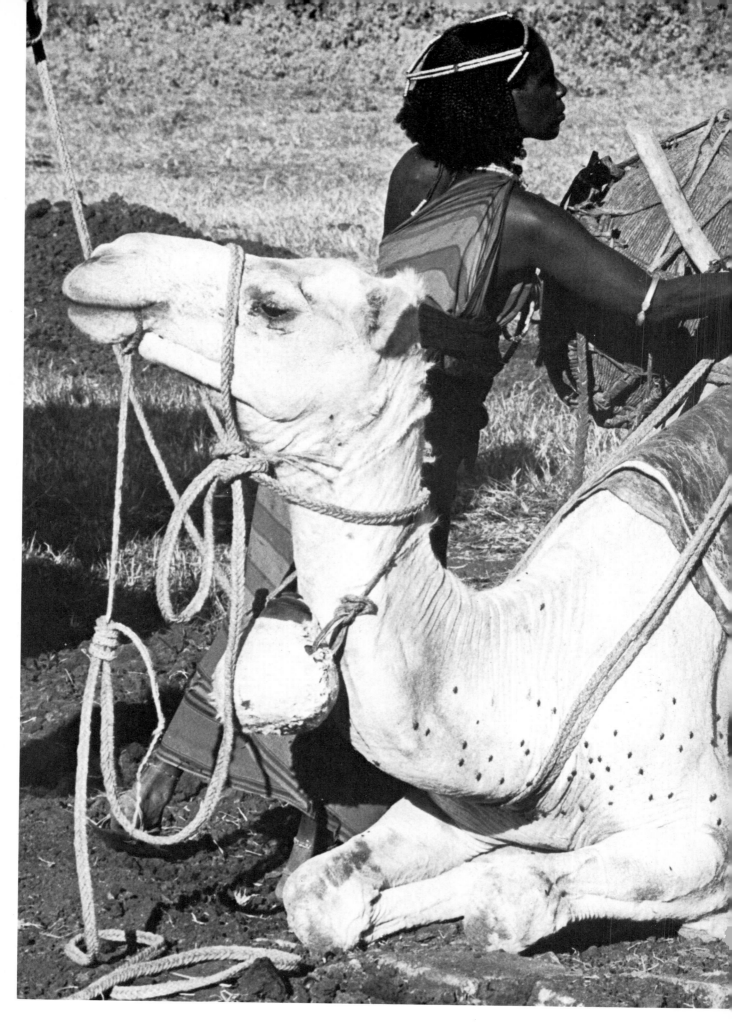

His *dubo* hat shows that this Gabbra man is part of the *Dabela* class responsible for many ceremonial duties in the traditional festivals

Left A Gabbra woman loading water containers on to her camel at the wells on Marsabit Mountain. Having walked on to the mountain in the morning she will now return fifteen miles into the desert to avoid night mists which sometimes give camels pneumonia

Overleaf A lovely Gabbra woman wearing aluminium jewellery made by local blacksmiths from old cooking pans

The Future

WEST OF KORR, at the edge of the Hedad desert, a broken windmill stands on the open plains. The stumps of its shattered vanes hang uselessly, like withered limbs, whilst the hot incessant gale whines through the metal framework. On one side two metal tanks stand empty on a concrete plinth where once they brimmed with water, drawn from a deep borehole by the spinning vanes. Now the tanks resound and boom in the rushing wind; around them an empty space of naked ground forms an open circle in the desert scrub, the soil beaten into sterile dust by thousands of hooves which came and went in the brief lifetime of this modern waterpoint. From a distance the mill and tanks stand sentinel in the empty desert, monuments to a good idea that failed.

'I am waiting,' said the District Commissioner at Marsabit, with quiet irony, 'for the scientists to tell me why all the waterholes are in the worst places.'

Of course the mechanism is well-known: a new pump which gives clean water attracts many customers in the desert. Marching their stock to-and-fro they quickly damage the root systems of the scrub and grass around the well, so that even after heavy rains there is no recovery. In the next dry season they must march further to reach adequate grazing, thus enlarging the sterile circle which grows cancer-like year by year.

It is bad enough around a solitary borehole; but often there are other factors which exacerbate the problem. The borehole may support a mission or a school, a police post or a hospital, perhaps all of these and then a tiny *duka* (shop) or bar. Around such foci people settle, a village grows, the stock increase, the pounded soil turns to dust and blows away. The settlement becomes a slum where beggars wearing handouts from the mission pluck the arms of travellers to ask for sweets and cigarettes, or shout 'pitcha, pitcha!' in the hope that someone will pay them twenty shillings to stand at attention, wearing a ridiculous overcoat, to be photographed.

This phenomenon, now referred to as 'the disaster of sedentarisation' by scientists who study desert areas, has been created with the best of good intentions often by dedicated individuals who have devoted years of patient toil, trying to improve the lot of the nomadic tribes.

Only now, almost a hundred years after Teleki and von Höhnel struggled through the deserts to Lake Turkana, are there signs that modern man with his science and technology may be able to offer effective changes to the pastoralists. If I have the temerity to write critically of developments in northern Kenya it is only after listening to the views of many workers who now have doubts about the wisdom of well-meaning schemes they have striven to implement. Hopefully with the benefit of their hindsight future workers can do better.

Change in the desert is uniquely intractable as many failed schemes and degraded areas testify; some of the reasons for this are physical – the remote, difficult country is truly a harsh environment – but there are other philosophical and psychological difficulties central to the problem of improving life in the desert which have all too often been disastrously ignored.

Two fundamental points: firstly, for much of the time pastoral-

Dust fills the air over the main street of Wamba in Samburu country. Here is the reality of 'development' in nothern Kenya: corrugated iron shacks and desertification

ists enjoy their way of life and only give it up if they are forced to, by some personal disaster like the loss of all their herds; indeed many who have found other work eventually return to the desert after earning enough money to buy new animals. Secondly, the only way to be self-sufficient in semi-desert country is to be a nomadic herdsman. Schemes such as the fishing co-operative at Kalokol on the western side of Lake Turkana, or the growing of irrigated crops near the Kerio river are peripheral to the real problem; there are 108,000 square miles of semi-desert country in northern Kenya and it is time more resources were directed towards helping the 800,000 nomads who live there to become better pastoralists instead of trying to make them give up their pastoral way of life.

Of course to argue that the traditional desert societies are perfect and should be left unchanged would be romantic nonsense. But it would be equally mistaken to argue that modern change is always for the better and there is much romantic nonsense talked about development. Nairobi's high rise skyline may be a symbol of success but the city also has its shanty towns and it is all too easy to exchange rural poverty for urban poverty. Only the merest handful of men from the desert tribes successfully move into a comfortable life 'down country'. Most finish up in very low-grade jobs, perhaps as night watchmen spending their days in the slums and their nights on concrete pavements, dreaming of their father's herds and longing for the taste of camel milk.

Too many youths who have been to mission schools in the desert finish up leaning against the verandahs of squalid shops in centres like Kargi or Maralal; their semi-education disqualifies them from their own society without giving them a viable alternative, and their brothers who were apprenticed in the camel camps may well be better off. In any case Kenya's severe problem of population growth (four per cent per year) means that there is already a surplus of young people without jobs in developed Kenya; there is certainly no room for yet more migrants from the desert.

One problem has been that we simply did not know enough about desert life to offer suitable training. Perhaps this is why there were hardly any schools in the north of Kenya until after independence in 1963. But when schools were started they offered a low-grade form of the same programmes being followed elsewhere in Kenya. Thus children are taught English nursery rhymes (translated into Swahili) and the usual 3R's syllabus at an age when they would normally have been herding goats and learning the traditional fables of their ancestors. No doubt all societies blunder forward and we must expect mistakes in the inevitable trial and error process. But the starting point (and aims) are so radically different in the nomadic tribes that I cannot believe a primary (or secondary) education modelled on European lines is the right approach.

Apart from education too many attempts to improve things have boomeranged and made them worse. Health care produces an increasing human population in lands already stretched to the limit of their carrying capacity. One Catholic priest proudly told me that his mission hospital had reduced the infant mortality

179

rate from 80% to 20%; I am torn between admiration and hopelessness. What will the extra 60% eat? At Kalokol, on the west side of Lake Turkana where there is a successful fishing co-operative employing Turkana people, the biggest health problem is venereal disease, imported by workers from southern Kenya.

This type of conundrum is typical of northern Kenya where cruel twists of fate seem almost pre-ordained to produce disaster out of helpful aid. Apart from cancerous desertification around the waterholes other things can and do go spectacularly wrong. A different priest described to me how the huge corrugated iron roof of the new technical school in Marsabit revolved in the sky above his head after being torn off by a whirlwind just before the school opened. In another incident an expensive fishing boat, which had been taken by trailer to Lake Turkana across the Chalbi Desert, dragged its moorings at Loiengalani and broke up on an island before it could be used. At Katilu an earth dam on the Turkwell river burst; the flood washed away roads and topsoil leaving the land worse than before. 'Shauri ya mungu,' (it is the will of God), say the elders and shake their heads with 'I told you so' conservatism.

The same conservatism allied to modern veterinary science has increased the problem of overgrazing. Traditionally the nomads have insured against drought and epidemics by increasing their herds as much as possible. Better a hundred half starved beasts than twenty high grade animals, especially as a man's status is judged by the number of his stock, not their quality. Now this philosophy worked when the human population was smaller and the losses due to raids and epidemics were greater. Today with diseases like rinderpest under control the preference for numbers over quality causes yet more overgrazing which adds to the desertification problem.

Some scientists have argued that a contributory cause of overstocking is the biological inefficiency of using milk as the basic diet. No other animal which is a secondary user of vegetation depends on milk; other secondary users are predators such as lions who eat meat – a much more effective way of benefiting from the grass eaten by someone else. Because of their dependence on milk pastoralists manage their herds in order to achieve high numbers of mature females (about two and a half times as many as on a modern beef ranch). If there are only normal losses such a herd can double itself in four years: to remain level it would be necessary to sell off 35% per year, which is far more than pastoralists do sell. So the numbers leap dramatically during good years only to crash at the next drought when, because of the large numbers, there is no reserve grazing to carry them through. If only they could be persuaded to sell more animals the cash could be used to buy grain and the average family could live on half the present number of animals.

Unfortunately in many areas the cattle buyers are entrepreneurs from southern Kenya who drive very hard bargains; so the pastoralists only sell when they are desperate, which means in a dry season when the land is already overgrazed, the animals are thin and the price of grain is high. Thus the herdsmen feel swindled and their reluctance to sell is reinforced.

Over all the impression is a depressing one of proud peoples caught in a slowly closing trap sprung by biological malpractices and ineffective aid. But in Kenya at least the trap is not yet shut and considerable efforts have been made to find an escape route. A recent wide-ranging multidisciplinary study established jointly by UNEP and UNESCO has added greatly to the fund of knowledge about desert life. This Integrated Project on Arid Lands (IPAL) used part of the Rendille and Gabbra ranges as its study area; but the intention was to discover solutions to the problems of semi-desert areas which can be applied world wide.

The complex plan which emerges involves many changes; but significantly they involve changing pastoralism, not eliminating it. The numbers of animals must be reduced and pastoralists must learn to sell off their animals regularly, so they need a proper marketing system which gives them a fair return. They must learn to eat alternative foods bought with the proceeds of these sales, thus reducing their dependence upon milk.

Damaged desert lands must be reclaimed by re-planting with desert shrubs and grasses. Badly damaged areas must be fenced off so that they can recover; and it may be possible to introduce exotic species of desert plant which will prove nourishing to domestic stock.

A vital factor is to improve security in northern Kenya so that herders can take their animals into areas they now avoid through fear of raids from other tribes. A major fault in desert societies is their failure to come to permanent terms with their neighbours. According to the IPAL study 40% of their area was unused because of this problem!

If all these aims are achieved then it will still be necessary to plan for droughts. In desert environments periodic droughts should not be regarded as unexpected disasters but rather as an inevitable fact of life for which plans must be made; there should be either stores of food or money in the bank.

Given all this it is technically possible for the shepherds of the desert to continue to live in their vast and spacious lands. Will Kenya's modern government and the many interested international agencies have the skill and persistence to get the message across in time? There is no place for a broad education on European lines. What is needed is a new type of education, specifically aimed at helping the nomads understand their own ecology. The whole thing should be done in the vernacular languages, for it must reach everyone, not merely those who speak English or Swahili. It needs good quality films, mobile presentations, touring lecturers and intensive training schools. What an adventure if it worked! A total of 630 million people live in semi-arid lands; someone must find a real solution to their problems. It would be appropriate if a start could be made in the land where the IPAL team made their findings and where man's most ancient bones are found. Will the traditional societies themselves prove able to adjust in spite of their inbuilt conservatism? Some would doubt if any fruitful change can come from outside a society; but having inflicted the hypodermic needle and the borehole on the pastoralists the developed world has an obligation to help them find a way through.

For myself, I feel privileged to have been able to catch glimpses of ancient ways of life whilst I travelled through the semi-desert lands. Are we all nomads in our hearts? Is this why we long for holidays abroad, weekends away from home and envy those who have the courage to throw up everything to sail around the world? Perhaps it is in our genes, this urge to find new lands; certainly I feel I need to know there are still places, somewhere in the world, where it is possible to wander in the wind.

And so I admire the shepherds of the desert. 'There would I go too,' my sub-conscious says, shaking off the desks and telephones, striding across the empty landscape towards the golden sun.

Long may they roam.

Photographic notes

For years when friends have asked me what kind of photographic equipment I use I have replied that the most important item was the Land-Rover. A weak joke perhaps, but I calculate that I have travelled over 15,000 miles in northern Kenya and it goes without saying that the whole of this distance has been off the tarmac, much of it on barely visible tracks; so a strong reliable vehicle has been an essential asset.

But for the technically minded all the photographs in this book were taken on 35mm Asahi Pentax cameras with Takumar lenses. For me the speed and ease of handling of 35mm cameras gives them a tremendous advantage over larger format equipment and in view of the very high quality of modern films I think it is a waste of time using anything other than 35mm for this type of work.

No doubt a dozen other makes of camera would have given equally good results but I would like to pay tribute to the reliability of my Pentax equipment which never let me down in spite of high temperatures and very rough journeys in vehicles, on foot and by camel.

Although I possess a motor driven camera I used it very rarely in northern Kenya since it makes the camera look (and sound) more impressive, thus making it more difficult to persuade people to let one take pictures. Throughout Kenya it is essential to ask permission before attempting to photograph people and one could easily get into an ugly situation by neglecting this simple courtesy. Since we always travelled as a family the presence of my own children was a major asset for they helped to create a feeling of trust. It would often break through the initial reserve if I photographed my son (or asked him to photograph me), thus proving to the onlookers that this technical gadget called a camera is harmless.

Even today, off the main tourist tracks, many Africans have never seen a camera and one can imagine the fears such an obviously sophisticated piece of equipment may inspire in the minds of illiterate people who have not seen one before. It often helps to let them look through the viewfinder when they especially enjoy long telephoto lenses; but I have met people who even refuse to look through the eye-piece because of their fear of the unknown. Not that I blame them! If someone from China arrived in my garden and started adjusting some highly complex equipment and pointing it at me . . .!

Although amateurs frequently ask questions about equipment they rarely ask which film one uses; but in fact this is perhaps a more crucial question. For colour I use Kodachrome 64, for black and white Ilford FP4, rated at ASA210 and developed in

183

Paterson's Acutol developer, using the compensation technique of greater dilution and longer development time to control the strong contrast of equatorial African light. We carried a small refrigerator in the Land-Rover (which could run off both the car battery and gas) which served for both food and colour films as temperatures were often 110°F (43°C) in the shade.

I always use two camera bodies and shoot as many subjects as possible in both black and white and colour. For scenic shots I like to try a polarising filter for colour and often use a polariser in tandem with an orange filter for black and white. My favourite lens for portraits is the 105mm and for landscapes the 28mm; but I often forget which lens I used for a certain shot and never believe those photographers who list the stops and exposures set for each frame. I think they make these up when they get home!

Of course the best light in Africa is early morning and late afternoon. At mid-day the vertical shadows are a disaster and it is best to put the camera away. Personally I do not favour automatic cameras and prefer to interpret the through-the-lens meter readings for myself; leave the automatic camera alone and it will produce the same skin tone for Africans and Europeans in close up portraits!

In the end, although good equipment is essential, the best photographs will be taken by photographers who think about the shots they are taking – something no amount of automation can do for them.

For the photography in this book I used four Asahi Pentax 35mm camera bodies and nine Takumar lenses:

17mm	f4	105mm	f2.8
20mm	f4.5	150mm	f4
28mm	f3.5	300mm	f4
50mm	f1.4	500mm	f4.5
50mm	f4 macro